MIKE PARROTT

SPORTS DEVOTIONALS

Team Huddles

ISBN 1-929478-11-9

Cross Training Publishing
317 West Second Street
Grand Island, NE 68801
(308) 384-5762

Library of Congress Cataloging in Publication Data in Progress.
Sports; devotionals; youth ministry; discipleship and evangelism

Published by Cross Training Publishing,
317 West Second Street
Grand Island, NE 68801

DEDICATION

To my athletes at home: Lindsey, Luke, Laurie, and Dan. Thanks for your help along the way. May these athletic and life principles continue to be found in you.

ACKNOWLEDGEMENTS

There have been a number of individuals who have made this book a reality and have knowingly and unknowingly helped me along the way.

First, I thank the Lord for all the students who have applied these truths and for the Lord who enabled them to see that they do work. Several of these students are mentioned throughout the book.

To my fellow workers John Karraker and Dave Livingstone whose efforts in pioneering the weekly team huddle strategy with students from their schools led me to develop the progressive talk strategy found in this book.

A special thanks to Walt Snyder whose heart for his athletes made it possible to see hundreds of students impacted with these team huddles.

I greatly appreciate the help John Lanzone has given me in bringing this work to completion.

My heartfelt thanks to my wife who encourages me in my student ministry and has always supported me while I was and continue to be involved in giving these weekly talks to students—even when it has made me late for dinner.

CONTENTS

A Strategic Perspective

It has been said that the pen is mightier than the sword. But today I believe that the value of what a writer puts down in print can easily be lost if its connection to real life is not seen by the reader. This book is not just words on a page. It is a dynamic tool that has, is, and will change students from the inside out. It is in light of this that I want you, the reader, to see clearly the different ways this book can be approached and used.

Devotional Tool

You can use this book as a personal devotional. Simply read one chapter a day and then spend time looking over the *Time Out* section at the end of each chapter. You will need a Bible and a pen for this part. After you have discovered the truth of the *Time Out* take some time to think about how it applies to you personally. Then thank God for who He is and His work in your life. Commit yourself to be God's servant after completing each devotion. Finally, take time to pray for others. Pray that they will learn the truth you just learned and that God will help them apply it in their own lives and that they will commit themselves to Him as His servant. When you finish the twelve huddles and the *Time Out* sections in the book turn to Appendix Two. Here you will find an additional nineteen *Time Outs* so you can make this last for a whole month!

Outreach Tool

Letters and words on a page may change your life personally, but God's words were meant to change other's lives too. God wants to use you as His mouthpiece to bring His message of truth and hope to your friends and fellow athletes. Take some time to read over the Introduction in this book and Appendix 3 in the back about using this book as an outreach tool.

If you want to see your friends reached for Christ, your peers become more open to spiritual truth, and you can identify with the truths from these lessons, then don't keep them to yourself.

Let your light shine and explore how you can use *Team Huddles* as an outreach tool. God may start a spiritual revolution on your campus just because you took these huddle talks to your own teammates!

Discipleship Tool

When God starts reaching your friends and teammates for Christ someone needs to step up and help them grow as new believers in the faith. You can be the one God uses to help your friends and teammates grow and mature in Christ! If you have already used this as a devotional then you already have learned exactly what a new believer needs to know to grow and mature in Christ—besides what it takes to become an athlete of excellence. Turn to Appendix 5, "Using *Team Huddles* As A Discipleship Tool," and learn how you can gather students together in a small group or in a one-on-one study of the Bible using this material. You will not be the first student to see his friends and teammates share the joy of growing together in knowing Christ and applying these huddle talks in their team competitions.

These team huddles are based upon biblical truth. In the *Time Out* section you will be able to see the Bible passages that talk about the principles you learned from each Team Huddle.

Since each huddle is based upon God's truth, it must be empowered by Him to be applied with constant success. A teammate who is not a believer may attempt to make use of each principle through a determined mental attitude and experience some outward success. God's truth always works. But at some point there will be frustration, I believe, for the one who does not know Christ. This is because he is separated from the power source that makes it possible for these principles to be consistently applied with both the right internal motives and the right external actions. This will give you the opportunity to let your teammates know of the importance of knowing God personally. Not because it will personally benefit their attitude and actions as an athlete, although it most certainly will, but because it will allow them to have fellowship with all who know God, it will bring them into an eternal relationship with God, and it will bring joy into their lives and your own life!

Remember, God empowers what He prescribes. So as you walk through these huddles seek to depend upon Him and His power alone to live out these principles. He wants to live His life through you.

Are you ready to meet personally with God? Are you ready to improve your athletic performance and become all that God wants you to be? Then you are ready to begin this team huddle adventure. May you experience all He has for you!

Introduction

"Let's bring it in!" yells the coach. Another practice is over except for a few comments the coach has for you. What he says in the team huddle is very important. It sets the tone for the next practice and game. What you do with it will determine whether or not all the practice sessions have helped you and how well your team does in the game.

In the next few pages are several team huddle challenges that have been given to hundreds of student athletes since 1974. While a few teams have only heard one of these talks in a single season, most of the football teams I have spoken to since 1985 have heard these talks at the rate of one a week during their sport's season. Have they helped any students? Yes! Here are a few comments from some students over the years:

"I always play better when I come to the team huddles after school."

- a junior in Pennsylvania in 1988

"Now I know that what you said is true. I'll never forget it."

- a senior in Ohio after winning their toughest game in 1992

"I wish we had these while I was playing."

- a senior in Oregon in 1975

Perhaps Tim said it best. After making 11 touchdowns during his senior year, being voted King of his Senior Prom, and competing in the State track meet, he had this printed in his school yearbook by his name instead of any of the above accomplishments:

"Even youths grow tired and weary, and young men stumble and fall; But those who hope in the Lord will renew their strength. They will soar on wings like eagles." Isa. 40:30-31.

During Tim's football season 21 of the varsity players discovered what 12 of the other varsity players already knew. There is a spiritual dimension to our lives. And in the team huddles they came to at Tim's house the night before each game, they all discovered how to start and develop this area of their lives during that one Fall football season.

Their team took the championship that year. Other teams have ended up in the state playoffs. Some teams have improved their records in their league. But most important, all the players who applied these team huddle challenges became better athletes, students and individuals and many were prepared for a joyous eternity.

What happens to you will depend on what you do with what you read. If the most that happens is that you become a better player, student and individual would you really mind? More importantly, you will have discovered how to start and develop an eternal relationship that affects you here, now, and on into eternity.

Enjoy the adventure!

1

Set Your Sights Beyond This Season

Lets go back to 1924. On November 1st of that year Montana State was playing Billings Tech. Frosty Peters, a freshman at Montana State, broke away from the Billings' defense and ran down the field untouched. Then, to the fans surprise, he stopped within 10 yards from the goal and casually drop-kicked the ball through the uprights. A certain six-point touchdown had become only a three point field goal!

As Frosty came off the field the coach seemed completely satisfied with what had happened. The next time that Montana had the ball a pass receiver stopped short of the goal line in what was another certain six point touchdown. On the next play Frosty drop-kicked the ball for three points.

Now the crowd knew something was up. Team members were all playing on the same page too. Frosty drop-kicked twelve more times in that half and made seven of them. In the second half the same pattern continued with Peters making eight for eight in just over one quarter of play. Peters left the game after bringing his total to 17 of 22. At that point Montana State was leading 51-0. Then the team was allowed to go on for touchdowns.

What had happened? Before that game the national record

for drop-kicks in a game was held by a high school player who made 15 in 1915. Frosty, his coach, and the entire team had the goal in this one game of having Frosty break the national record.

Sometime ago I was asked if the drop-kick could still be used today. As a matter of fact, Joe The Toe, was the last one in 1949 to use the drop-kick in a football game. But, according to NFL rules (11.3), the drop-kick is still legal.

What goals do you have for your next game? What is your team goal?

Value of Goals

Think about these statements:
"A goal is something toward which you aim."
"Goals are the specifics of what we want to accomplish."
"Goals are powerful motivators."

Jim Irwin, former Apollo 15 astronaut, once said, "Decisions determine destiny." What you decide to focus upon, what decisions you make, and what becomes your pursuit will determine your future.

Your focus is critical to your future. Ice skaters will focus upon one spot each time they spin around again and again to maintain their balance. A former Olympic Diver never tucked. Why? Because he understood that where your head goes your body will follow. What you focus on is where your body will go.

Tests done on people to better understand weightlessness and motion sickness in space have discovered that if the person has no point of reference to look at they will get sick! This was discovered by placing volunteers in a machine which had spinning walls. Anyone inside had nothing to focus upon and would feel a lack of stability in this environment.

I recently saw a statement on the trailer of a truck which said, " Safety is our goal." No matter what we do goals are important. What is your goal for this game? This season? After this season? You need something to focus upon from game to game.

It also makes a difference as to the kind of goals you set. Are you aiming for a better team record? Do you want to improve your personal stats? Do you have a goal to win the next game? Or is it your goal to become the best player you can become?

If one of your sports is football you could aim for more tackles or hurries on the quarterback, if you play the defensive line. As a quarterback you could strive for more completions, better fakes, and better hand-offs. Perhaps your goal is more interceptions, more receptions, or running your pattern faster. No matter what sport you compete in you need to set goals. However, you must decide before the game what you intend to do.

Some of us tend to think we are getting better when all we are doing is shooting arrows at a barn and then drawing the target around the arrow after it hits the barn. Don't just set a general goal, be specific. If you play football, *decide as a team* to gain 200 yards rushing and over 100 yards passing in one game. Change the goals if they are over or under what your team can do. *Decide as individual players* on three sacks, two interceptions, ten tackles, or 15 completions. Make it specific and then adjust your goals if you achieve them early in the game.

Limitations of Short-range Goals

Many years ago one U.S. Olympic team coach felt that there must be some limits to human strength, speed, agility, and endurance. So he developed a list of his "ultimate" track and field performances. "No one, said Brutus Hamilton out of confidence based upon long experience, would ever run the 100-yard dash in less than 9.2 sec. or the mile in less than 3 min. 57.8 sec. No one would ever put the shot more than 62 feet, throw the discus more than 200 feet, do better than 7 feet 1 inch in the high jump, 27 feet in the long jump, or 16 feet in the pole vault."[1] But since then, more than 40 years have passed and every "ultimate" record has been broken. Many wondered if Bob Beamon's long jump record of just over 29 feet would ever be broken. It too has fallen. Many expect a recorded jump over 30 feet to be the next long jump record!

If you think the goal is out of reach you will naturally let down. Winning more games may be a desire but it is not an adequate goal. Some teams have a lot of good players. Others have improving players and one great player or a few of them. Should every team have as their goal to win more games? Or should every team have a goal that each player improve as a person to become all he can be? If your goal is to win more than last year and you reach it early in the season you may relax instead of moving ahead with new goals for the season.

What will happen when you play weaker teams if your goal is only to beat the other team? Jerry Kramer writes in his book *Instant Replay* that the Green Bay Packers had a difficult time being up in games with weaker opponents.[2] The tendency is to not practice as hard or take the game as seriously as you would an unbeaten team. Obviously this hurts your development as a player and as a team.

What happens if your goal is to improve your personal stats? Again, you will let down emotionally, mentally, and physically if you only aimed at reaching that goal instead of hitting it and moving on to more challenging ones. Being ready to adjust your goal is important, but the fact that you will probably have to adjust your goal at some time should not keep you from developing goals.

What happens if you are way ahead of another team? Do you still strive to reach more challenging goals? If you settle on only winning the game you will stop playing at your potential and "watch out" because that is when you become vulnerable to injury on the field and sudden defeat!

Goals that reach beyond the season

Decide to play for goals that will develop you as a player and person not only in your sport but beyond it. Relate your short-range goals to a goal that will reach beyond this season and the game itself. You need a goal that all other goals will relate to. Remember, your immediate goals are determining your destiny!

In the movie "Chariots of Fire" the lives of two Olympic athletes are portrayed. Harold Abrahams has as his goal an Olympic gold medal. During his pursuit he meets Eric Liddell. It seems that his quest is very uncertain as Liddell is very fast. But as the Olympics arrive Harold finds himself as the only Britain in the 100m. Eric has had to drop out and has been rescheduled for the 400m. As Abrahams finishes the 100m having reached his goal of receiving a gold medal there is a great emptiness within him. He now has nothing to aim for and there is no joy even in his victory. Instead, he is disillusioned.

Eric, however, who due to his personal convictions to not run the 100m qualifying race on a Sunday, was forced out of the race and now prepared to run the 400m. He was not use to running that distance. Even as he trained for it his times were disappointing at best. But on the day of the race he ran the race of his life and outran his closest competition by several strides. Eric set a new World Record and received a gold medal. His reaction to winning was much different than Abrahams. His running in the Olympics was just a short-range goal that he had to do on his way to his life-long goal. For Eric there was joy in winning. He had no regrets about his decision to pull out of the 100m race.

Why the difference? Eric had a life goal that reached beyond the games and time itself. His goal reached on into eternity. That goal was a powerful motivator throughout his entire life. This goal made even the short-range goals more satisfying for him.

Take a minute and think about your personal goals for being in this sport. What goals do you have? Are they clear to you? What team goals do you have? Now think beyond this season.

How far will your goal get you in life? Do you have a goal that will reach beyond this season? You can discover the goal that Eric knew and aimed for during his life. Eric spent his entire life in pursuit of being pleasing to God in all that he did. But you must know Him *before* you can please Him. Why not take a minute and consider your relationship with Him?*

Father, I want to know you and establish my goals so that they reach beyond this sport's season. Thank you for helping me do this.

*You can discover what motivated Eric by reading the material in the back entitled, "Starting an Eternal Relationship."

1 Paul Lee Tan, Encyclopedia Of 7,700 Illustrations: Signs Of The Times (Rockville: Assurance Publishers, 1979) p. 776.

2 Wes Neal, The Handbook on Coaching Perfection (Milford, MI: Mott Media, 1981), p. 49.

TIME OUT
Making Your Spiritual Life The Priority

1. What sports do you compete in at this time?

2. What is one goal you have for your current sport?

3. What are some of the things that we can boast about according to Jeremiah 9:23?

4. What should we boast about according to Jeremiah 9:24?

5. In Philippians 3:4-6 the apostle Paul says he had several things he could boast about, but in Philippians 3:7-11 he says they were nothing when compared with what?

6. What area of your life should be your top priority? (Circle One Answer Below)

   Physical   Social   Mental   Spiritual

7. Read Philippians 3:12-14, what did Paul see as his top goal?

Before we can develop our relationship with God we need to begin a relationship with Him. If you don't know Christ personally turn to Appendix 1 and read

"Starting An Eternal Relationship."

If you know Christ, think about what you value most. In light of the verses you have looked at in this Time Out, what adjustments to your goals do you need to make?

2

What Me? It Wasn't My Fault

In 1929 the University of California played Georgia Tech in the Rose Bowl. California was leading 7 - 6 when Roy Riegels picked up a loose ball. He saw his teammates behind him blocking the Georgia Tech players and took off for the end zone. The crowd became louder as he ran. He thought that they were encouraging him to run faster. But they were yelling, "Wrong Way! Wrong Way!" Benny Lom, one of the team's fastest backs, also cried out, "Roy, Roy, stop!" But Roy kept running. Benny took off after him and caught him at the twelve yard line. But by the time Benny brought him down they were at the one yard line. California was forced to punt but Georgia blocked the punt in the end zone scoring a two point safety. In the locker room Roy was discouraged. But when the coach announced the starters for the second half Roy couldn't believe it. The same guys who started the game would start the second half! During the second half the Georgia Tech players felt that Roy played harder, hit better, and gave more than he had given in the first half. But in the end the victory would go to Georgia Tech and the margin of victory would be the two point safety.

There will always be plays that we would like to call back and run over. We can decrease the number of mistakes we make by studying the game plan, knowing our routes, assignments, and the blocking schemes. We can even envision ourselves doing these things right. We can prepare right with a good night's sleep and eating the right things the day before the game since we play the game on the previous day's energy that we have stored up. But when we blow it, we still have to deal with it. How quickly we do this will determine how fast we are back playing at our full potential.

Have you ever made a mistake on the field? We all do. We miss an assignment, don't read the play as it develops, or fail to react quickly enough. There is an athletic term that describes these failures. It is a term that you have probably heard in a different setting—sin. Sin is an athletic term. It was used in archery to describe the distance between the center of the target and where an arrow actually hits. It is the distance between perfection and our true performance.

OK, I did it. Now what do I do?

In high school I played ball with a guy who bothered me when I first met him. It seemed that he never made mistakes, instead it was always the others who made mistakes. That bothered me until he surprised me during our big rival game. Marty called the play in the huddle. It would be the double reverse. The ball was to go from Marty to me and then I would give it to Charlie. Charlie then had the option of passing or running with it. After Marty hiked the ball he came towards me to make the hand off. He put the ball out for me but as I began to clamp down on the ball he decided to pull the ball back and try to run around the corner with it. But the ball never got back into his hands, instead it ended up on the ground but we recovered it. As

Marty came back into the huddle he apologized to me for trying to change the play and causing the fumble. That was freeing for me. I didn't have to think about it anymore. I could move on and get ready for the next play. Guess what play we called in the huddle this time? The double reverse again. This time the ball came to me and I got it to Charlie, but as he received it his knee hit it and there the ball was on the ground again. Again we maintained possession. I told Charlie I was sorry for my hand off to him. In the huddle Marty called the same play again. This time the ball came to me, and I got it to Charlie. Although the play made some yardage it left us just short of a first down and so we had to kick it away.

What Marty had learned and I had also discovered was that you can recover from mistakes quickly if you simply admit them to yourself first. Then you need to admit them to the one you offended. Did you catch what I just said?

First, Admit the mistake to yourself.
Second, Admit it to the one you offended.

What if I don't want to admit it?

One wise man once said, "He who conceals his sins does not prosper, but whoever confesses and renounces them finds mercy." (Proverbs 28:13) When we fail to admit our errors we actually lose energy to play the game and to live our lives. We actually begin to build a barrier between us and other people. A famous leader of a country wrote about this affect upon himself sometime ago. He said, "When I kept silent about my sin, my body wasted away through my groaning all day long." "My vitality was drained away as with the fever heat of summer." (Ps.

32:3,4) When was the last time you walked out of an air conditioned home into a muggy and hot summer day? How did you feel? Did you feel your energy zapped by the heat? That is what the above statement says happened to David, a leader of a whole country when he didn't admit his sin. He didn't have his normal reserve of energy to do his work. Also he didn't relate well to his most loyal followers and continued to make more mistakes with them because he would not admit his previous mistakes. Eventually a friend confronted him and got him to admit his faults. But several relationships had already been damaged. One could not be restored. That is what happens to us when we hold things inside and fail to admit our mistakes to ourselves and others we have hurt.

Besides finding mercy, maintaining a reserve of energy, and developing healthy relationships, another benefit of learning to admit our faults to ourselves and others is that we will develop a healthy view of who we are. Do you have the freedom to accept yourself for who you really are? You don't have to hide your faults! You don't need to use up energy trying to rationalize or ignore them. You can accept yourself, admit your mistakes and move on!

Will I keep hearing about what I did?

When Colorado played Missouri in 1990 it came down to the final seconds of the game to decide who would win. With time running out the quarterback deliberately threw the ball into the ground to stop the clock. On the next play Colorado scored making it 33 - 31 as the game ended. As the tapes were looked at later it was verified, Colorado had intentionally thrown the ball into the ground on their fourth down. Then they were given a fifth down which enabled them to score and win the game. The game's score was not changed. Colorado defeated Missouri by using a fifth down play!

Our mistakes may be recorded in time but they don't have to continue to be a weight around our necks the rest of our lives. We can have freedom from their influence on us. If you fail to admit that you do make errors you will struggle every time you make a mistake. You will spend your energy on hiding it, blaming it on others, trying to rationalize it away when it comes to mind, and you won't be free to be yourself or focus upon what you are supposed to be doing.

We all need forgiveness. It is one of our four basic needs![1] When was the last time you asked someone you hurt to forgive you? Have you ever asked your coach to forgive you for the mistakes you have made on the field? If you have you probably did not get yelled at by him, but instead you received valuable instruction on how to improve and keep from making the same mistake again. However, we may not always receive immediate forgiveness from those we hurt even when we honestly and humbly admit our mistakes to them. Why? Because they are human. It may take time for them to forgive. But there is someone who will always forgive you when you come to Him. He will give you the forgiveness you need to keep going. He will forget your faults and never bring them up again! He will give you the freedom to be yourself so you can focus on your role and responsibility in the game and in life.

Alfred Anderson was playing for the Minnesota Vikings on their special teams. On the game's kick off the ball came to him. But he could not control it and fumbled it. In order to deal with the situation he determined in his mind not to let it happen again. When the other team kicked off again it also came to

Alfred. Again he fumbled it! As he walked off the field to face his teammates and the coach he paused and looked up and caught a picture of God looking down upon him saying, "It's OK. You know I'm always with you." And even though he was hurting on the outside, there was real joy inside him. He was assured that God accepted him as he was. He always forgives.

Just before a key high school game between two teams ranked in our city's top ten, the quarterback of one team talked with me on the phone. He said, "I was just getting ready to call you. I wanted you to pray for me about this game. I keep remembering the mistakes I made in the game last year. How do I deal with it?" We talked about his need to study the plays he was weakest on, picturing the play going right, and getting a good night's sleep. But even if something goes wrong you can recover quickly and not allow it to keep you from doing your best for the rest of the game. Why? Because you know the one person who stays with you for every play. He only had to keep the communication lines with Him open. Just admit your faults to Him too. He will forgive you every time. After the game Jason said, "I never felt such energy in a game. I'm convinced now of His presence in my life."

Isn't this what you need?

Take a minute to think about your response to your mistakes on the field and in life. Are you lacking energy for the game and life? It may not be a mistake in a game that is robbing you of your energy and focus. It could be a problem you have with your parents, a teacher, your employer, your girl friend, or your best friend. How are you dealing with it? Do you waste energy rationalizing your mistakes, blaming others, or trying to forget them?

Are you free to be yourself in front of others? Can you admit it when you are wrong? Can you admit it to others you have hurt? Are you in communication with the person that Alfred Anderson and the high school student knew? Is there anything between you and Him?

You know what you need to do. The big question is, "Are you doing it?" Take a minute now to deal with anything that has come to mind. Admit the fault to yourself. If you hurt someone else, decide and plan to admit it to them too. It may be your coach, one of your parents, a friend, or God. Don't waste your energy hiding it. Deal with it now.

Father, thanks for providing the way to deal with my mistakes and to set things right.

[1] Bill McCartney, et al., What Makes A Man? (Colorado Springs, Colorado: Navpress Publishing Group, 1992), p. 20.

TIME OUT
Experiencing God's Love and Forgiveness

If there is any unconfessed sin in your life you can make things right with God right now.

1. Who do we hurt when we sin? Look at Psalm 51:4

2. How does unconfessed sin affect us? Look at Psalm 32:3,4

3. In light of question two, what affect can unconfessed sin have upon your athletic performance?

4. What do we need to do to deal with our sins? Psalm 32:5

    (Confession means agreeing with God about our sins. It is turning from them to Him and choosing to do what He wants you to do.)

5. What will God do when we admit our sins to Him? Psalm 32:5

    Remember, confession of sins (missing the mark of God's holy character and conduct) needs to be done as soon as we become aware of the sin. Take time now to ask God what you need to confess to Him. Then do it. Finally, thank Him for forgiving you and removing the guilt of your sin. Read I John 1:9 and Psalm 103:12.

Anytime you become aware of an attitude or action that is displeasing to God simply take a moment to confess it to Him and by faith in His word (I John 1:9; Psalm 103:12) thank Him for forgiving you and cleansing you from all unrighteousness and impurity.

Trust God to forgive you and give you the power to live differently!

3

Motivation that Lasts a Life Time and Beyond

What are the top five questions football players have while sitting on the bench? After some thought, here are a few. In fifth place, "Who did you say was having a party?" In fourth place, "Do you think we will get in the game this week?" In third place, "Did we just change in the girls locker room?" In second place, "I thought we played them last week?" And in first place, "Does Pizza Hut deliver to the bench?" But seriously, what keeps you coming out every week, being hit by others, taking care of injuries, and disciplining yourself to get out on the field and play again? Why do you continue to play any sport at all?

Motivations

There are many things that can motivate you. One may be a girl friend—or a potential one. In 1931 there was a game between UCLA and the University of Oregon which was motivated by a girl. Mike Frankovich of UCLA and Bill Bowerman of Oregon had several things in common. They were both quarterbacks for their teams. They also both played as defensive backs. Finally, they also had the same girl friend. And before the big game she said that she would choose the one on the winning team.

In the fourth quarter Oregon had the lead 7 - 0. That was when things became interesting. Mike Frankovich moved his team in for a score. Then his roommate, Pants Livesay, missed the extra point. That made it 7 - 6, in favor of Oregon. Bill Bowerman then took his team down the field towards another score. Bill threw a long pass and guess who intercepted it—Mike Frankovich. After the change of possession there were only seven seconds left in the game but Frankovich now had the ball. On the next play He threw as hard as he could and the ball headed straight towards—Bill Bowerman. But just before Bill intercepted the pass, guess who showed up? Pants Livesay—the one who had missed the extra point. He ran in front of Bowerman, caught the ball, and darted into the end zone as time ran out! Both UCLA and Mike Frankovich won that day.[1]

A relationship with a girl may motivate you for one game but what happens when you are not on speaking terms, what about when you break up, and what if she doesn't like your sport? You need more than this to stay motivated for a whole season and the rest of your life!

Your coach can also be a strong motivation for getting your act together and playing hard. While in school I had an injury that took me out of my sport. There was a big meet coming up that I had really hoped to run in. I wasn't thinking that I would be ready for it. Then, to my surprise, my coach showed up at my door as I was home recovering. He just dropped by to see how I was doing. After that I was determined to try to get ready for the track meet which was only two and a half weeks away. A coach can motivate you to go for it. I did well but it only helped for one meet.

Some people are motivated by locker room talks. Knute Rockne felt that his team needed some extra inspiration as they came into Atlanta to play Georgia Tech. While in the locker room with his team he said to them, "I have one wire here, boys, that probably doesn't mean much to you, but it does to me." As his voice started to crack he breathed deeply and said, "It's from my poor sick little boy Billy, who is critically ill in the hospital." Then with trembling lips and watering eyes he read Billy's wire, "I want Daddy's team to win."[2] The team was so moved by what they heard about the coach's son that they roared from the locker room and ripped apart Georgia Tech 13 - 3. When they returned home to South Bend, Indiana, a cheering crowd of 20,000 greeted them. Guess who was jumping around in front of the team as they got off the train? Billy—the coach's son. Knute had sent the telegram to the team himself.

In another situation, a University of Michigan football coach gave such an inspiring half-time talk to his players that he forgot how they came into the locker room and ran the team out the wrong door and right into the swimming pool! A couple of them nearly drowned before they could be fished out.[3] Locker room talks can help motivate you if they are done right. But it only helps you for that one game—and maybe only for that half.

There are many other motivations for playing the game. Revenge—working to beat a team you lost to last year. Anger. Hatred. Money—but you don't have to think about this one in high school. Scouts—maybe you know that a college scout or pro scout is in the audience and you are playing with the hope that he will notice you. You may even play a game hoping it will lead to a scholarship from a college or a better chance in the college draft! But if it doesn't come you may become very discouraged—especially if you were the best in your position but not considered big enough for playing college ball or professionally.

One student told me that when he came to the team's motivational meetings (team huddles) that he always played better!

Limitations

While you may experience many of these motivations none of them will help you become the person or athlete that you are meant to be. They are temporary. Many of them will help you start strong but will quickly zap your emotional energy for the game—often by half-time! You need motivation that will take you through the sport's entire season and continue for a lifetime.

Lasting Motivation

There is only one motivation that can do that. It is a commitment to a person. But not just any person. That person must be one who is always there, who never changes, who always accepts you the way you are but cares about you too much to let you stay where you are, and motivates you to give 100% all of the time.

Years ago there was a college freshman at Ohio State who discovered this type of motivation. He started out on the 5th team—it was known as the scout team. The first two games of the season were at home. He was permitted to dress for the game, but since there was not enough room in the team hotel he had to stay in his dorm room. During the last quarter of the game the coach called his name. He put on his helmet, ran out, and on the second play they gave him the ball. The line opened up a hole you could have driven a truck through. He ran for it, and without being hit, he fumbled the ball as it was pitched to him and the other team recovered it. He felt totally discouraged as he walked off the field to face his teammates and coach. He was only in the game for one and a-half minutes. And he had not officially carried the ball at all.

He visited his father the next day who put things in perspective for him. He reminded him of the commitment he had made earlier in life to a person who was always there, who never changed, who accepted him as he was, and that prepared him for the next week.

The second game was also at home. Again there was no room in the team hotel for him, but he was allowed to dress for the game. Half way through the first quarter the coach called his name. He was caught off guard. This was completely unexpected. In fact, since he was a freshman and Coach Hayes was not yet sold on a new rule allowing freshman to play varsity, he thought it was a mistake but the coach kept calling for him. Finally, with great excitement, he ran out on the field without one very important piece of equipment—his helmet! He had to run back to the sidelines in front of more than 86,000 people in Ohio Stadium, get his helmet, and run back into the huddle. In the huddle they called his number and in the next three and a half quarters he set the all-time single game rushing record at 239 yards for Ohio State as a fifth string scout tailback. He went on to became the only man in history to win two Heisman trophies. His name—Archie Griffin.

When he ran off the field that day to his teammates and coach, he stopped in front of them and more than 86,000 people and knelt at the out of bounds line in a prayer of thanks to the person who had been his motivation for that game. When he got up he lifted his index finger and did it every time after that when he carried the ball. Was he saying Ohio State was number one? He could have been saying that but he wasn't! Archie was saying that the person who he played for, who was always there, who never changed, who accepted him as he was, and who was giving him the motivation to play, He was number one in his life![4]

One high school student in Pennsylvania made eleven touchdowns his senior year. On the eleventh one he broke through the line 46 yards out and told me later, "All I could think about was getting there as fast as I could and kneeling down in the end zone to thank the one who made it possible." During his senior year he was also elected King of his senior prom and competed in the state track meet. When he wrote the words that he wanted to appear under his name in the school's yearbook, he didn't list abbreviations of all the things he had done. Instead he wrote, "Even youths grow tired and weary, and young men stumble and fall; but those who hope in the Lord will renew their strength. They will soar on wings like eagles." Isa. 40:30-31.

Do you have motivation for a lifetime? Are you committed to a person who is always there, never changes, accepts you just as you are, and motivates you to play at 100%? Take a minute and think about what is motivating you right now. Will it last? Do you know the strength and motivation that drove Archie in the game? Why should you be committed to Him? Because He gave his life for you while you were not even interested in Him.

Father, thank you for making it possible for me to know you. I depend upon you for my strength and motivation for all I do.

---

1 Wes Neal, The Handbook on Coaching Perfection (Milford, OR: Mott Media, 1981) p. 86.

[2] Bruce Nash and Allan Zullo, Bernie Ward. ed., The Football Hall Of Shame (New York: Pocket Books, 1989) p. 59.

[3] Bill Stern, Bill Stern's Favorite Football Stories (New York: Doubleday and Company, Inc., 1950) p.112-113.

[4] Adapted from a talk given by Josh McDowell at "Something's Happening, USA" in Minneapolis, Minnesota over Labor Day 1989; Dave Newhouse, Heisman, After the Glory (St., Louis, MO: The Sporting News Publishing Co., 1985) pp. 275-276.

TIME OUT

Responding to God: Power for Living

1. From Philippians 2:12, what are we to do as believers?

    To work out our salvation means to allow what God has done within us to surface and become how we think, feel, and act. It is simply allowing God to have His way in our lives.

2. Does God have His way in your life at this time?

3. What is God doing in you according to Philippians 2:13?

    God is working into our lives the desire to do what He wants and the ability to do it!

4. Why is He doing this? Look at Philippians 2:14-16.

5. God works in you through His Holy Spirit. According to Ephesians 5:18 what does He command us to do?

6. When we trust God by faith to fill us we will obey His word and experience several other things mentioned in Ephesians 5:19-21. What are they?

7. God is at work in you right now if you know Him personally. Once you have committed your life to Him and confessed all known sin, God is ready to empower you with His strength to be Christ-like in all you do. Simply ask Him to fill you and thank Him that He has done so by faith in His word (Eph. 5:18) and His promise as God (I John 5:14,15). Take a minute now to ask Him to fill you with His Holy Spirit.

To be filled with the Holy Spirit is to be empowered and controlled by God's power. We experience this as we by faith surrender every thought, desire, and decision to our Lord. We let Him have His way in our lives. We then experience His power to live the Christian life. Remember: Only Jesus Christ has ever lived the Christian life. You can only live it as He lives His life through you! (See Gal. 2:20 and Appendix Three – Developing An Eternal Relationship With God.)

4

Character: Who You Really Are!

Workouts for football had just begun. I had played for the last two years but this would be my first year with helmets and shoulder pads. In junior high we only played flag football. Now, as a freshman, we had all the equipment. My first practice was going well until the coach called me over. The coach told me to bend down, and said to the rest of the team as he held my head and helmet under his arm, "You break 'em, we'll replace 'em." I had split my own helmet right down the center. "Go get yourself another helmet," the coach said. So with my helmet in hand I was off to the storage room. In the storage room there was a large pile of helmets kept in a large wooden bin. I began carefully looking through the helmets. I found some that were too small, some too big, and some that fit "OK," but none that were just right. Finally, after feeling that I may be taking too long to look for one, I settled on one that was "OK" and ran back onto the practice field.

You don't have to be a freshman to face new challenges. But a freshman often has more challenges to deal with than all those steady and experienced upper classmen, right?

Since you are still growing when you are a freshman and your body is undergoing some big changes, you may be a completely different athlete from when you were in junior high. And as a result you may be asked to change positions on the team. You may even experience a fair or unfair amount of kidding from upper classmen. You may also find that you have to learn many new plays and details about playing the game that you never thought about before. Your health can change. You may have to overcome an injury to continue to play. But how you handle all these changes will make a big difference in your life. It will determine your character.

The Priority Of Good Character

Coach Bill McCartney, former head football coach for the University of Colorado, said that character is the number one quality that he looked for when he recruited students for his football program. Surprisingly, most coaches put character at the top of their list!

John Wooden, former UCLA basketball coach, once said that you need to be more concerned about character than reputation. Why? Because reputation is what others think you are, character is what you really are. Character is who you are when no one else is watching you. Someone has said that character is what you would do if you could get away with it and no one would find out about it.

Vince Lombardi said, "Character is the direct result of mental attitude." Your character is shaped by what you think about and believe.

Developing Good Character

There are three qualities that determine your character. First, your convictions—what you firmly believe to be true. Second, self-control. Once you have a firm view of what you value as right and wrong the next step is developing self-control in that area. Third, perseverance. This is repeating over and over again successfully the area you have been working on and trying to control. Perseverance is the ability to be self-controlled in an area over time and through difficult situations.

When I volunteered to coach for my son's soccer team as he was growing up, I knew that I needed to be careful not to lose my temper over a player who missed his assignment. I needed to help him improve. I still needed to be firm, but I had to work on being patient with the players. That didn't come easily for me in the heat of the game. But it helps to know that others have experienced the same thing.

In his rookie year in the NFL Ray faced an unusual opportunity to demonstrate his character. Ray was surprised that he had been drafted into the NFL. But after the excitement of being picked to play there was the reality of training camp. He now found himself blocking and tackling veteran players. There were many times during the camp that he was taunted as a rookie. Then an unexpected opportunity to show what he was made of occurred in the dining room during training camp. Ray had sat down to eat as the chant began. "We want a rookie, we want a rookie,...." He hoped his name would not be called. But, when his name was called he knew what he had to do—sing a song to the entire group while standing on top of a chair.

As he stood up he asked if he could dedicate his song to someone. The veterans had never had anyone dedicate a song to another person, but they decided that he could do it. Ray then dedicated the song to a veteran he had met earlier who had continually taunted him about being a rookie.

Ray stood on the chair and sang, "Jesus loves me this I know, for the Bible tells me so...." He did not sing this to mock him. He didn't do it to be mean. No, he meant it. He had a genuine concern for this fellow athlete. And this was what gave him confidence as a rookie. It also demonstrated that he had developed strong character.

Character only comes as we have firm beliefs, practice self-control in those beliefs, and persevere. Self-control does not come without some work. There are many challenges that can cause us to lose control.

In a recent high school soccer tournament Loveland was playing Hamilton. As the game went along it became clear that Loveland would prevail. One of the Hamilton players had just received his second yellow card and was out of the game. There was only one Loveland player between this player and his bench. As the Hamilton player walked towards the bench he decided to pick a fight with the unsuspecting Loveland player. The fight resulted in the Loveland player receiving a broken nose. But surprisingly the Loveland bench did not clear. They kept their wits or composure and remained calm and seated. The Hamilton players and coaches were so embarrassed by the actions of their player that they forfeited the remainder of the game. The Hamilton fans quietly walked out of the stadium embarrassed too. The Loveland player did recover enough to return to play the next tournament game. And a huge lesson had been learned.

Self-control affects whether or not we exhibit good sportsmanship or not. If we fail to demonstrate self-control we can embarrass ourselves, our families, our coaches, and our schools. It is not just getting control but maintaining it that is critical.

Swen Nader once played basketball for the San Diego Clippers. Basketball players often have rough on the road schedules during the year. As he spoke to a few of us along with a defensive guard from the San Diego Chargers, they both agreed that professional sports was a very difficult place to live life. You are under the spotlight day and night. "How would you do if a TV camera followed you everywhere you went?" they asked. Then they mentioned something I had not heard any other athlete say before. They both asked us to keep them in our prayers because of their desire to be faithful to their wives and families. "While you are on the road, night after night, there are plenty of women hanging around the hotel rooms looking to spend the night with just one of the players." they explained. Both of these guys didn't want what was being offered, but to be confronted with this night after night on the road was a constant challenge to them.

I'm always disturbed when I hear of members of a professional sports team being accused of immoral conduct. We never seem to hear the complete story from the news media. We hear of the accusations with players even being specifically named. But when a player's name is cleared from the list we won't find that on the front page or at the top of the news story. Here is what we miss. In a 1991 case, several members of a professional football team were mentioned by name for immoral conduct while in Seattle for a game. But what you would not have known is that one of the players called a close friend of his before the story even came out and literally cried to him while on the phone because, whenever the media picked it up and whatever might be said by the media, he did not want his friend to think that he had been a part of what had taken place. He wanted his friend to know that he was a man of integrity. I can tell you that that player had nothing to do with what took place because his character could be trusted. I'm sure that some of the team members were wishing that they had been more self-controlled. But this man and others who had been falsely accused had to patiently wait for their names to be cleared of any wrong doing. Wouldn't you rather stand with a clear conscience before the public even if falsely accused? You can, but you need to deal with your thoughts. You need to maintain self-control.

Pursue Good Character

Who you are is eventually going to surface in your actions. A wise man who was king over a nation a long time ago once said, "As a man thinks in his heart, so is he." Who are you really? What are you like when you are alone? Do others know the real you or do they only know you by your reputation?

In school my friends said I was "cool." I thought it was great. But, the more I thought about what it meant to be cool, the more I disliked the term. It could have meant that I lacked firm beliefs and thus real character!

Are you confident? Can you stand alone? Are you the same when no one is watching? If not, you can be. One of the reasons we aren't ourselves is that we have not dealt with the spiritual dimension of our lives. I believe that many of you would like to have firm beliefs, be self-controlled, and persevere in the right convictions. But a lack of character and lack of strength to carry out those beliefs can be traced to not dealing with the spiritual dimension of one's life. A philosopher once said that we would be restless all of our lives until this area was taken care of once and for all.

Take a minute and think about who you are. Do others know the real you?

Do you hold firm convictions that are good and true for all? Do you need to develop firm beliefs, better self-control, or the ability to persevere? Is the spiritual area of your life together so you can do this? You can be a man of character.

Father thank you for helping me become the person I should be.

TIME OUT
Learning To Walk With God

1. Read Proverbs 23:7a. What causes people to act the way they do?

2. Since a person's actions are determined by what they think about, what do you spend your time thinking about?

    How will this affect what you do?

3. Knowing Christ allows us to develop self-control in His power. Look up the following verses and answer the questions:

    2 Peter 1:4a - What has God done for you?

    2 Peter 1:4b - What do His promises allow us to do?

    2 Peter 1:5-7 - What are we to be diligent to work into our faith? (Note 7 qualities)

    2 Peter 1:8 - Why are these qualities important?

2 Peter 1:9 - What has happened if a believer lacks these qualities?

Would applying I John 1:9 to their lives help them get back on track?

2 Peter 1:10-11 - If you practice these things what will be true of you in verse 10?

In verse 11 it says that our capacity to enjoy heaven with Jesus will be affected by whether or not we practice these qualities. Remember, character is the result of practicing God's Word (exercising self-control) over time. He has the power to do it. Trust Him to live His life through you today.

4. Take a minute and let God again point out to you any area of your life that is not pleasing to Him. Confess anything He shows you. Then ask Him to fill you with His Holy Spirit. Trust Him by faith that He has done what you have asked of Him.

5

A Will to Prepare

Although many thought he was too small to play college football, he did not think so. Robert had his sights set on playing for one team and one team only—The University of Notre Dame. But his physical size was not his first hurdle towards his goal. He lacked the grades to get into the school after completing high school. Although disappointed in not being accepted he did not lose sight of his goal. He prepared to achieve his dream by attending a junior college. But when he applied to Notre Dame again he was again turned down. With only one more opportunity to get in he studied hard and when the final time came to apply he did and this time he was accepted. He had set himself upon a course of preparation both academically and physically so he could get into the University of Notre Dame and become a walk on for the football team.

During his first season he worked harder than the rest of the players and earned a spot on the team the starters played against in practice. His entire two years as a football player at Notre Dame was spent on the practice squad. As the players were listed for each game during his final year in college he kept waiting week after week to see if his name was there. When it came to the end of the season and he was still not listed as playing he could have easily given up. But finally, in the last game of his senior year he was given the opportunity to suit up and take the field with the team. He wasn't expected to get into the game but even that took place towards the end of the game. His story has even become a movie simply called, Rudy. His name—Rudy Ruettiger.

Bobby Knight, basketball coach from the University of Indiana once said, "It's not the will to win but the will to prepare that is important." Rudy had prepared for years to play at the end of one game at the end of a season at the end of his football career. Whatever sport you compete in will require preparation mentally, physically, and spiritually.

Mental Preparation

In high school I enjoyed running track. But my events were mainly field events. However, I was almost always scheduled to run the 440 yd dash. Today it is the 400 meter run. My times were disappointing at best. And it seemed that for this event I had mentally decided that I would never actually be competitive in it. But the more I thought about it, the more dissatisfied I became with settling for less. Could it be a training issue? I worked hard at improving how I ran and even learned a few things that helped. Although it was towards the end of the season in my senior year I gave it all I had in my final 440. In the first 100 yards I was still with the other guys, then at the half way point I was out in front. Now the doubts came. Why was I out in front? I had never been here before. Are the other guys still running? Was there a second whistle signaling a false start that I had missed? Am I the only one out here running? I was mentally losing it and the discussion in my head got the better of me and between the 200 and 300 yard mark in the race I took a quick glance behind me to see my competition right on my heals. That glance back cost me a lot. My mind had been clearly focused but now in the midst of doubts I had lost the drive that had catapulted me into the lead. In the final 100 yards I would be passed by most of the runners and I had to be satisfied with finishing in the pack but not place. Although this was my best finish in this race it was little consolation for what could have been if I had stayed mentally focused on the race and had not lost confidence along the way.

Preparation for the game begins with a will to prepare for it. Every day in practice is an opportunity to become a better athlete and a more disciplined person. Remember, talent can only get you so far. Eventually you will be surpassed by others who are working hard to improve their skills and abilities if you are only relying upon your talent to compete in the game. Before practice prepare yourself mentally. Be willing to work hard. Know the benefits. Realize it will take time to improve. But don't miss out by not determining to do your best even in practice.

Physical Preparation

Reggie White, perhaps the best defensive player to ever play, once was asked by a kid how he got his strength on the football field: "Do you pray for it?" he asked. Reggie replied, "Sure I do, but I know the only way God will give me maximum strength on the field is to get in the weight room and then out on the track. We can't ask God to give us something if we're not willing to work with all our might to receive the best."[1]

Once you have determined mentally to play the game and practice hard you must then do it. This will mean a lot of physical exercise and training. But you need to understand a few things about this process before you start.

Muscular strength is critical for an athlete. "Muscles are where energy is released, power is produced, and where movement originates," according to Ellington Darden, Ph.D., author of dozens of fitness books. "In addition to being the engine of the body, muscle is also the shock absorber. Strength enhances the integrity of the joints, guarding against painful tears in the connective tissues of the knees, neck, shoulders, elbows, ankles and—above all—the lower back."[2]

Therefore, preparing your muscles for competition is very important. But to do it correctly you need to warm up your muscles even before you begin to stretch and definitely before working out. This can be done by jogging until you have developed a light sweat. What happens is the jogging increases the flow of blood to your muscle tissues and increases their flexibility and lowers your chance for injury. After this you should stretch out all muscle groups that will be used in your sport. Then begin your workout and strength training.

Your willingness to prepare correctly will increase your strength and lower your risk of injury both in preparing for the game as well as during the game. You need to seek out advice from your coaches as to the specifics of your personal workout and strengthening program.

Spiritual Preparation

In the forward of Deion Sanders book titled, *Power, Money, & Sex,* T.D. Jakes states, "Anything sought other than God will always leave us strangely depleted and deeply disappointed."[3]

Deion Sanders had it all. But success almost ruined his life.

Why? Because wealth, power, guy-girl relationships, and fame still leave people empty inside. Deion says, "After scoring touchdowns and dancing in the end zone, after a stadium full of cheering fans had finally gone home, I was still empty inside."[4]

We need to begin and develop the spiritual side of our lives. This is the part that puts all the others in their proper place.

Father, help me develop the spiritual side of my life. Make me the person you want me to be.

[1] Terry Hill, Going for the Goal (Nashville, Tennessee: Broadman Press, 1990), pp. 11-12.

[2] Terry Duschinski, "Benefits of Weight Training," New Man, September/October, 1994, p. 78.

[3] Deion Sanders, Power, Money, & Sex (Nashville, Tennessee: Word Publishing, 1998), p. x.

[4] Ibid. p. cover

TIME OUT
Living For God

1. How should we mentally prepare for anything we do according to Col. 3:17,23,24

2. From these verses (Col. 3:17,23,24)
   - who should you play sports for?
   - who should you do your homework for?
   - who should you do your job for?
   - who should you do chores around the house for?

3. Take some time and give to the Lord all that you now do and should do. What things do you need to let Him control? What things do you need to do for Him instead of for yourself, your parents, your coaches, your employer, your teachers, etc?

   List them here and then ask God to help you with each one:

6

Mentally Alert

Back in the days of George Blanda and Joe Namath, there was Ray. You probably have not heard of him. He played for San Diego State and was drafted by the Oakland Raiders. During his football career he knew what it meant to be mentally alert.

As his team prepared for one particular game, the team's scouts had made a key observation on their opponent. When number twenty-three came into the game the team only ran three different plays. One play had him lining up on one side of the field and the other two plays had him on the other side. Ray's team developed a special defense just for when twenty-three was in the game. Ray called the special defense as number twenty-three came into the game. Then he watched as twenty-three lined-up on the side where he could run two different plays. However, the scouting report had even noticed that you could tell which of the two plays were about to be ran depending upon how he placed his feet as he lined up.

Ray had played long enough to become familiar with the cadence of the quarterback and positioned himself towards the hole in the front line that he knew would open up for their running back—number twenty-three. As the quarterback called out the signals Ray timed his move just right to hit the hole in the line just as it opened up. He met number twenty-three just as he received the ball. Ray hit him, picked him up, placed him on his back in the back field. He knew it was a good hit as he heard him expel all his air as he hit the ground.

This tackle was the result of good scouting and good execution. They had been alerted to exactly what the other team would do. They had all the information they needed to respond correctly and do the right thing on the field.

What would have happened if they had not noticed that number twenty-three was in the game? What if they had not prepared a special defense just for him? What if they had not noticed that how he lined-up gave away the play he would run? What if Ray did not know that a hole in the line was about to open up for twenty-three to run through? And what if Ray had not timed the quarterback's cadence just right to hit the line as it opened?

You need to be at your best mentally if you are going to play the game with skill and power. You cannot ignore the scouting report and hope to get by. You need to know it and respond to it. That means you need to be focused on what you are doing. You need to be there 100% mentally, 100% emotionally, and 100% physically.

Your Early Warning System

How can you be sure that you are alert mentally and not ignoring the information you have received? If you're not there 100% mentally, 100% emotionally, and 100% physically there is a way to know it. You have within you a built-in warning system that is also a reliable decision-making tool. It takes into account what you think, feel, and do. When what you *do* does not line-up with what you *think*, the alarm goes off. Also, when what you *feel* doesn't match the *facts*, it sends you a warning signal. This tool you have is your conscience. It is a reliable tool as long as you use it rather than rationalize or ignore what it tells you.

If Ray had failed to respond to that information he would have missed the opportunity to make a key play. His usefulness to the team depended upon him responding to what was true. How you respond to your conscience will make the difference as to whether you are alert on the field or not.

Sometime ago Craig was drafted by the Chicago Bears and then traded to the Minnesota Vikings. He had made the initial cuts and was on the traveling team. During a game he was hit and brought down. There was a burning sensation in his arms as well as a feeling of numbness. For a few seconds he could not move his arms. This had happened before, but he had not thought much about it. However, this time he decided he would ask the trainer about it. He felt awkward about mentioning it as he thought it was probably not that important anyway. But the trainer decided the matter needed to be looked into. Craig went in for x-rays and waited for the results. When the doctor told him the results he couldn't believe his ears. He had a hair line fracture in a vertebra in his neck. He had a 50-50 chance of being paralyzed from the neck down with any hit in the game. At that point his professional career ended. Craig has become success-ful in another career today. But where would he have been if he had not listened and responded to the report by the doctor?

Some high school and college athletes are trying to play the game without listening to the facts. They are ignoring the warn-ing signs of their conscience and playing the game anyway, but they are not playing at 100%, 90%, 75% or even 50% of their ability because they come on the field on something, under the influence, or even pre-occupied with having compromised their morals. All of these will drain a person's strength, cause him to lose focus in the game, and keep him from the mental alertness needed to take advantage of the opportunities in a game to make those key plays.

I have given this talk to several teams in Ohio and Pennsylvania. In almost every situation I will have someone come up to me at the end and tell me that they have experienced exactly what I just told you. One student said, "When I get hit my arms go numb, they get warm, and I can't move them. I thought everyone experienced this when they got hit." I told him he needed to see his doctor. Another student said, "I know guys on our team that have played in games drunk or on something." That's sad because they hurt themselves and the team's performance. Others have said, "I know what it is like to compromise my morals and then try to play the game. It is always there in the back of my mind occupying my thoughts and keeping me from focusing on the game."

Making The Opportunities Count

A former president of the United States once said, "Opportunity is like a horse. It gallops up and pauses for a moment. Then it gallops off." Teddy Roosevelt was the president who said that. If you are not there 100% mentally, 100% emotionally, and 100% physically you can miss the opportunity when it comes.

Sometime ago I met Bob. He was 6'6" and 225 pounds. His dream was to be a walk on for Denver. He had been training to prepare to walk on and try out for the team. When I met him he had just missed the time to walk on for that year. He was then preparing for next year. Yet every year that went by he never walked on. He had one problem that has kept him from fulfilling his dream—drinking. His lack of discipline in his personal life became the obstacle to him stepping onto the field and fulfilling his dream. Today his dream is over. His opportunity has passed.

It is not only the game that is affected by not being alert, but your day to day life. If you are not living your life or playing your sport with 100% alertness you can change! You can live with a clear conscience. You do not have to ignore or suppress the warning signals it sends you. However, if you do your conscience will become numb and unable to warn you of coming trouble. It becomes like a burn victim who has had the nerves of his hand so damaged that he cannot sense when something is too hot to touch. He no longer knows that what he is doing is harming him.

You need to listen to the warning signs coming from your conscience. What is it telling you now about your thoughts, feelings, and actions? Are you focused on what you are doing? Are you 100% there mentally, emotionally, and physically? Which area needs help?

Putting It All Together

Alertness comes as we deal with all dimensions of our lives: the physical, mental, social, emotional, and spiritual. But the most important area is the spiritual. It is because of this dimension that you even have a conscience at all! If you put this area in order all the others will come into focus and you will be there 100% mentally, 100% emotionally, and 100% physically in whatever you do.

Take a minute and decide what area of your life needs the most attention at this time. Is it your mental, emotional, physical, social, or spiritual? Then I'll close with a brief prayer.

Father, thank you that you provide us with answers to those things that are keeping us from being there with 100% alertness. Help me to listen to my conscience and to develop the spiritual area of my life. I trust you to help me in these areas.

TIME OUT
Pursuing God With A Clear Conscience

1. What kind of conscience are we to maintain according to I Peter 3:16?

2. How do you deal with a guilty conscience? (Remember I John 1:9)

3. What can happen to the conscience if it is ignored according to I Timothy 4:1,2?

   What does a seared or callous conscience look like according to Ephesians 4:17-19

4. Developing your spiritual life means living a different type of life as a believer. Note how you are to live your life now in Christ from Ephesians 4:20-24:

5. According to I Peter 3:17 it is better that you suffer for doing what is right than for doing what is wrong. Think about these situations and decide how you would do what is right even though it may mean you suffer for it:
   A. Your peers want you to get involved in doing something that is illegal and you won't go along with it. What are some things they might ask you to do and how could you refuse to take part with them?

B.   You are pressed by friends to do something that can harm your body and make you less in control of your actions. What do you do?

What might your friends do if you refuse to go along with them? How should you respond to them?

C.   Read I Peter 3:18 and write in your own words why you should follow what is right and not be influenced by others to do what is wrong:

Remember, being mentally alert begins with a clear conscience and then responding to it as quickly as possible. You develop our conscience by learning what is right and wrong from God's Word. Read 2 Peter 3:17,18.
What are you warned about here?
What are you encouraged to do?
How can God's Word help you according to 2 Timothy 3:16,17?

Why not start reading God's Word daily? Begin with the Gospel of John in the New Testament and read a chapter a day. Simply wake up 10 minutes earlier in the morning, turn on a light and read a chapter before you begin your day. Write down the time of day you will read from His Word:

Write down the day you started doing this:

7

Know Your Coach

On December 11, 1978 Green Bay Packers coach Curly Lambeau was deep in thought about what to say to his team at half-time. They where losing 16 to 14 in the championship game with the New York Giants. If he could just make the right adjustments he could turn this deficit into a victory.

As the team ran off the field and headed for the locker room to await the coach's key words and revised strategy, Lambeau took some time in coming off the field. With the team out of sight the coach made a wrong turn under the Polo Grounds. "He opened the door to what he thought was the clubhouse and wound up on the street. Before he realized his error, the door slammed shut behind him." "Lambeau pounded on the door, but it did no good. Then he raced to the nearest gate. The security guard refused to let him in. 'If you're the coach, what are you doing out here on the sidewalk?' the guard sneered. Lambeau hustled off to another gate and another guard. But no amount of pleas or threats could get him in there either. The second guard shoved him away saying, 'Yeah, sure, and I'm the King of England.'"[1]

As the players waited for their coach they found themselves needing to discuss on their own what changes needed to be made, but they could not agree. "By this time, their angry, red-faced coach had charged the main gate, only to be stopped once again. Screaming at the top of his lungs, Lambeau attracted a big crowd, including some reporters."[2] The reporters immediately recognized Lambeau and convinced the guards that he was indeed the coach of the Green Bay Packers. However, the second half was about to begin by the time he reached the locker room. The Packers continued to come up short in the second half and lost 23 to 17.

Knowing the coach and taking the time to hear from him can make or break you as a player and as a team.

Listen To Your Coach

When Boddy Dodd was the athletic director at Georgia Tech he carefully instructed his quarterback in the last minute of play not to pass the ball under any circumstances. At this point Georgia Tech was leading 7 to 6. As Georgia Tech marched down the field with the ball and made it to the opponent's ten yard line, it seemed that they could do no wrong. At this point the quarterback was overcome by temptation. He passed the ball on the next play and it was intercepted by the rival team's fastest back. As he broke into the open field and raced toward the goal line he was overtaken at midfield by none other than the quarterback!

After the game, the losing coach remarked to Georgia Tech's coach, "I'll never understand how your boy overtook my fastest back." "Well, I'll tell you," came the reply. "Your back was running for a touchdown—my boy was running for his life!"[3]

Listening to the coach can definitely save you from unnecessary anxiety and difficulties. It can also keep you from being pulled from the game.

Some time ago during a game between Georgia Tech and Oglethorpe, coach Bill Alexander instructed his Georgia Tech quarterback to stop trying to score and to kick the ball. Georgia Tech was beating them badly at this time. There was no need to keep scoring or to give them a chance to get back in the game. However, Georgia's quarterback failed to listen to the coach and was quickly pulled from the game. A second quarterback was sent in with the simple orders to kick and not score. Again the quarterback didn't follow the coach's instructions. A third quarterback was then sent in by a now angry coach. As the third quarterback also failed to obey the coach a fourth one was called for and given instructions in no uncertain terms, "Go in and get that sap out of there! I want you to quit trying to score and to kick the ball. If you don't do what I say—so help me I'll throw you off the squad!" yelled the coach. The fearful young substitute wholeheartedly agreed to follow the coach's instructions to the letter. A few plays later the Georgia Tech team blocked and recovered a kick on the Oglethorpe one-yard line. On the first play from scrimmage with only a yard to go for a score the fourth quarterback for Georgia Tech called for a punt. He took the snap and kicked the ball completely out of the stadium. Then he turned to the bench and shouted, "See coach—I told you I can obey orders!"[4]

Although this story goes to an extreme to make the point it is still true that listening to the coach means that we not only hear what he says but we follow through with it. We actually do what he tells us to do! That can be hard but it is the right thing to do. He is the coach! Our role is to listen and obey.

Get To Know Your Coach

Unless you take time to get to know your coach you will never hear from him or benefit from his expertise.

A REAL COACH WILL INVEST IN YOUR LIFE

Archie Griffin, the only two-time Heisman winner, may not have attended Ohio State had it not been for the opportunity to get to know the coach better. In fact, he had been considering Northwestern instead.

Rudy Hubbard, an assistant coach under Woody Hayes, knew that Archie's parents had some concerns about how minority athletes might be treated at the college and arranged for them to meet with six African-American businessmen who had played football under Hayes. What they discovered was that Archie would be treated fairly at Ohio State. In fact, they discovered that Woody Hayes had a genuine concern for his players.

Woody continued to recruit Archie by having his wife take Archie's mother out to lunch. Then he visited his home and finally came to Archie's High School and locked himself and Archie in a room together for two hours just to show Archie that Ohio State halfbacks do carry the ball no matter how big they are.

A REAL COACH HAS EXPERIENCE TO LEAD

It has been said that leaders produce leaders. In the same way coaches produce other coaches. One man who learned coaching under Woody Hayes was Bo Schembechler. He became the head coach at Michigan. While at Michigan he recruited another coach to his staff, Bill McCartney. Bill would later become the head coach at the University of Colorado. When you spend time with a coach you learn about him.

When Bill hears the name Bo Schembechler he thinks about several things: "Like strength, leadership, grit, honesty—and yes, even humor." "Bo's philosophy, on the field and off, was basic and simple: Confront everything, ignore nothing." "The other thing he always stressed was team. Never the individual, but the team. He preached it night and day and I'm sure he got a lot of that from when he coached under Woody Hayes at Ohio State."[5] Bo was sensitive to the needs of individuals on the team and he was a good decision maker. When he recruited a player he told him the truth. He simply stated, "Let me tell you something, young man. I don't care what you've heard and I don't care what you've been promised somewhere else. Here's what I'm telling you. I'm not giving you anything, but if you really have the right stuff, it'll surface at Michigan."[6]

A REAL COACH WILL POSITIVELY IMPACT YOUR LIFE

When you get to know your coach as an athlete you benefit from the strength of his character. When Michael Jordan played for North Carolina his coach was Dean Smith. His influence upon Michael was noted by his father, James Jordan, before a 1993 play-off game in Chicago.

"People underestimate the program that Dean Smith runs. He helped Michael realize his athletic ability and hone it. But more important than that, he built character in Michael that took him through his career."[7]

A Real Coach Cares About Others

The 1961 Heisman trophy winner, Ernie Davis, had learned early in his athletic career the value of a coach. During his high school years he met Marty Harrigan. Harrigan was Davis' football coach. Their relationship began to develop as Davis would come to Harrigan for friendship and advice. The coach would counsel him as a father would his own son. And soon they had developed a family-like relationship. This unique relationship occurred at the right time for in just a few short years Ernie Davis would die of leukemia at only 23 years old and although he was drafted by the Cleveland Browns he never had the opportunity. The Browns chose to retire the number he would have worn, number 45, even though he never played for them.[8]

A Real Coach Knows How To Listen

When Larry Bird played for the Boston Celtics his coach K.C. Jones called for a time-out during a close game. Although he had diagrammed a play for them to do, Bird came back with, "Get the ball out to me and get everyone out of my way." With that the coach responded, "I'm the coach, and I'll call the plays!" He then turned to the other players and said, "Get the ball to Larry and get out of his way."[9] A coach knows when to listen, too. But the team needs to do what the coach calls.

You Need A Spiritual Coach

Bobby Bowden, Florida State's football coach, makes it clear who his ultimate coach is: "Football is not my number one priority in life." "It's a priority, a big one. It's the ability God has given me to make a living." "Everybody has a void in life. If you think you can find happiness by becoming a millionaire, I'm sorry." "Money's not gonna fill it. Fame's not gonna fill it. Neither is fun. You can only fill it with God."[10]

Are you a good listener? Are you getting to know your coach? Do you have someone who can coach you in spiritual things? Do you listen to and spend time with the person Bobby Bowden knows? You can, You should.

Father, teach me to listen to you and help me get to know you.

[1] Bruce Nash and Allan Zullo, The Football Hall of Shame: Nash & Zullo Publications, Inc. 1989), pp. 63,64.

[2] Ibid.

[3] Paul Lee Tan, Encyclopedia of 7700 Illustrations (Rockville, Maryland: Assurance Publishers, 1979), pp. 862-863.

[4] Bill Stern, Bill Stern's Favorite Football Stories (New York: Doubleday and Company, Inc., 1950), pp. 79-80.

[5] Bill McCartney, From Ashes To Glory (Nashville: Thomas Nelson Publishers, 1990), pp. 87,88.

[6] Ibid. pp. 89,90.

[7] John C. Maxwell, The 21 Irrefutable Laws Of Leadership (Nashville: Thomas Nelson Publishers, 1998), p. 75.

[8] Dave Newhouse, Heisman, After The Glory (St. Louis, MO: The Sporting News Publishing Co., 1985), pp. 178-179.

[9] Ibid. p. 49.

[10] Ken Walker, "The Wit And Wisdom Of Bobby Bowden," Sports Spectrum, October, 1993, p. 25.

TIME OUT
Knowing God

1. Who should we spend time with according to Matt. 6: 6,9

2. How do you listen to God (note Matt. 4:4; John 17:17; 2 Timothy 3:16,17)?

3. Spending time with God in prayer and in His Word should be a daily practice according to Matt. 6:11. In Mark 1:35 what did Jesus do?

    Why did Jesus pick a lonely and quiet place to pray?

    (Note the verses before and after Mark 1:35 to find out) According to Matt. 6:5-13 how should you spend time with God?

4. If you get to know God better and listen to Him what will be true of you?

    Isa. 40:28-31

    Daniel 11:32b

5. Determine to daily meet with God and get to know Him. Listen to Him from His Word and ask God for the strength to do what He shows you. Try adding these things to your time with God:

A. Begin your daily time asking Him to speak to you.

B. Read one chapter in the Bible. Begin in the Gospel of John and read the second chapter the next day and so on until you finish that book. Then start another book of the Bible: I John; Ephesians; I Thessalonians; Romans; Psalms; Proverbs; etc.

C. Take notes about what you learn that God is like and what man is like.

D. Note what God speaks to you about as you read. Thank Him for what He shows you.

E. Each day tell God what you have learned and pray for yourself and others who need to know or learn what He just told you that day from your reading in His Word.

8

Dedication: Living
by Principles

With five games to go in six days back in 1899 the University of Sewannee football team was undefeated. But the teams they were about to face were five of the most powerful teams in the country. And these teams were in five different cities a total of 3,000 miles apart!

Their first game was against Texas University. University of Sewannee won that game 12 to 0. The next day they traveled by horse and wagon with little rest—there were no cars, buses, or planes in those days. They beat Texas A&M 32-0. After another long ride by wagon they played their third game in three days. They trounced Tulane University 23-0.

On the fourth day they took time off to pray and rest as it was Sunday. The next day they played undefeated Louisiana State University and beat them 34-0. Finally, their fifth game in six days and their last game, they beat Mississippi State 12-0.

Not one team had been able to score on them! But more amazingly they did all this with 11 men and no substitutes! Also their college had less than 100 men attending it!

Developing Your Talent

When my wife and I visited France in 1988 we had the

opportunity to visit the Louvre—that large museum where there is painting after painting. One of the artist's works we saw were sculptures done by Michelangelo. (He was not one of the teenage mutant ninja turtles.)

Michelangelo is best known for his work on the Sistine chapel in Rome where he spent long hours each day painting on his back with his hands held up over him. (If you don't think this is an athletic feat just try holding your hands above you for a long time and work on something.)

He spent long days and often into the evening for four years (1508-1512) working in this position. But before attempting this project he spent a year (1505) on a gigantic sculpture made of metal only to have it melted down and made into a cannon after it was finished. Not a very encouraging thing to happen to a project that he had spent such a long time working on, right?

Why didn't he give up? Why didn't he decide to do some other type of work? How did he develop such dedication to his work? That's it. What made him dedicated to this work?

It probably came from his early years with his art teacher Bertaldo. As Michelangelo was working on a sculpture in the art studio and nearing its completion his teacher Bertaldo entered the studio. With a hammer in hand his teacher walked over to the sculpture that his student Michelangelo had worked so long and hard over and smashed the sculpture to bits.

Bertaldo then turned to his pupil and said, "Talent is cheap, dedication is costly."

As an athlete you may have talent, but without dedication to develop your ability you won't become an outstanding athlete.

Dedicated To Proper Principles

In 1988, Anthony Munoz and Howie Long were the best defensive player and the best offensive player of the year. A magazine wanted to do a spread on both of them on opposing pages. Anthony turned down the publicity, fame and money. Why? The add was sponsored by a beer company.

Anthony has now become the first Cincinnati Bengal inaugurated into the NFL Hall of Fame. Anthony is well respected in the Cincinnati community and throughout the athletic world. His name has been used by a local bank in Cincinnati for a weekly athletic scholarship for high school athletes. These athletes are honored for their athletic ability and community service with a $1,000 scholarship for college. Each March there are interviews with each of the weekly winners and one of the students will get a $10,000 scholarship to the college of his choice.

Anthony was dedicated to the game he played so well and that dedication continues today. As a result others want his name to be identified with their product. His reputation is the result of making hard-nosed decisions to be dedicated even if at first it may cost him an opportunity for greater fame and publicity.

Counting The Cost Of Being Dedicated

Could you have persevered with the U of S schedule? Would you have had the courage of your convictions even if it meant a lost opportunity? Perhaps not. But you can. You can be a man of conviction who is dedicated to living by principles. When a person has the spiritual area of his life together he has the ability to live by his convictions without failure.

In the days of Roman Emperor Nero there was a group of

men known as the Emperor's Wrestlers. These were fine, stalwart men, the best and bravest of the land, who were recruited from the great athletes of the Roman amphitheater.

In the amphitheater they overcame all challengers. Before each contest they would stand before the emperor's throne and proclaim, "We, the wrestlers, wrestling for thee, O Emperor, to win for thee the victory and from thee, the victor's crown."

When these men went with the Roman army to Gaul (France), many among their ranks began to embrace the Christian faith. Because of this Nero sent word to his centurion Vespasian that those who had done this must die.

The message was received in the dead of winter. Vespasian stood before his men and asked for any who had done this to step forward, 40 men stepped up. Being moved by how many had responded he gave them until sundown to renounce their faith. At sundown he again asked for the men to step forward who had embraced this faith. Again 40 stepped up, saluted and stood at attention. He then gave the order for the men to strip bare and move out onto the ice of the frozen lake all the way to the middle.

As they marched out they could be heard singing, "Forty wrestlers, wrestling for Thee,   O Christ, to win for thee the victory and from thee, the victor's crown."

As the night went on the voices grew faint. And as the break of dawn approached you could see one wrestler working his way back to the fires burning on shore. At that moment the song changed, "Thirty-nine wrestlers, wrestling for Thee, O Christ, to win for thee the victory and from thee, the victor's crown."

With that the centurion Vespasian shed his clothes, ran out to the group and sang "Forty wrestlers, wrestling for Thee, O Christ, to win for thee the victory and from Thee, the victor's crown."[1]

When Dave Johnson was in his senior year at college he discovered that he had natural talent in the track and field events. Although a delinquent teenager in high school, he was about to begin a path that would take him to the 1992 Olympics as a decathlon athlete!

His coach said, "This kid has energy. Natural ability. He runs strong hurdles. He's 6 foot 2 inches and 170 pounds." At that time he was introduced to the decathlon. As Dave's dedication to the sport and mental and spiritual principles developed he broke the school's decathlon record in only his second meet. But it would be the Olympics that would prove to be his biggest challenge.

In 1992 as Dave was preparing to compete at the Olympic trials he felt a sharp pain in his right foot. His friend Dan had not made the Olympic team and now Dave's position was in question.

The pounding of the trials only made his foot worse. At home he could not even train as the pain was so intense. An MRI showed that he had a stress fracture in the foot. Dave went to the Olympics determined to somehow endure the pain.

In his first event, the 100 meters, he regretted his decision. Halfway through the race he suddenly felt a stabbing pain in his right foot as if he had stomped on a dozen knives. On the second day during the hurdles he heard a POP and this pain brought tears to his eyes. The ankle had cracked more. Then, on the pole vault runway with the pole in his hands, Dave focused upon the image of Christ as he carried his cross. That was all he needed to finish the decathlon and take a bronze medal on a broken foot.[2]

Talent is cheap, dedication is costly. Do you have what it takes to keep going when the going gets tough? Do you know the mental and spiritual power that drove Dave Johnson, Anthony Munoz, and Michelangelo to develop and excel with their skills?

Think for a moment about these questions:

What are you completely, whole-heartedly committed to?

Is it worth that much attention?

Are you willing to pursue it no matter what the cost?

Remember, dedication is seen over time and through adversity. Are you demonstrating that you are dedicated to your convictions? Are your convictions worth being committed to?

What made these men excel? It was a result of inner strength that comes from developing the spiritual dimension of their lives. Your spiritual development is worth it. What have you done in developing this area of your life?

Father, direct my path so that I am a dedicated person and athlete.

[1] Andre Kole and Al Janssen, From Illusion To Reality (San Bernardino, CA: Here's Life Publishers, Inc., 1984) pp. 119,120

[2] Verne Becker, "The Spirit Behind Dave Johnson," New Man, September/October, 1994, pp. 21-24.

TIME OUT
Living A Sacrificial Life

1. Look up and read Matthew 26:47 to Matthew 27:66. What did Jesus choose to do and experience:

2. Why did He do this? Read John 10:7-18.

3. In light of God's love for us how should we live according to 2 Cor. 5:14,15

4. Read Romans 12:1,2. What should you do in light of all He has done for you?

5. Take some time to offer your life to God in a short time of prayer. Tell Him you want Him to live through you. Then commit yourself to daily live for Him and to allow your mind to be renewed with His Word.

9

Perfect Chemistry

It was one of those things that you find hard to believe unless you see it yourself! But there it was on the sports news on the evening of November 20, 1982. That day Stanford was leading California 20-19 with less than a minute and a half to play. And then the unexpected happened on the kick-off.

California's defensive back, Kevin Moen, received the ball on California's 45. He then lateraled to Richard Rodgers who continued down the field for ten yards before lateraling to Dwight Garner. Dwight then ran twenty more yards down the field and lateraled back to Rodgers.

Fans were already coming onto the playing field anticipating the end of the game. Even the band had ventured into the end zone. But the game continued as Rodgers lateraled to Marriet Ford who then lateraled back to Moen who had received the kick-off. Time had ran out as Moen ran through the fans on the field and into the end zone where he ran over one band member holding his instrument.

This perfect five-lateral return gave California a 25-20 victory over Stanford.[1]

What amazing alertness by each player to get into position to receive each lateral and to find an open path through all the defenders and the fans coming onto the field! This is working together as a team at its best.

Perfect Chemistry Doesn't Just Happen—It Is Developed

In the chemistry lab you have to pay attention to what you are mixing together and you have to do it in the proper sequence to get the desired result. Putting together a team that works together is a big challenge for any coach. One of the coaches who accomplished this was Coach Bear Bryant. When he retired from the game he held the record for the most wins in the history of college football. He said, "...I have learned how to hold a team together—how to lift some men up, how to calm others down, until finally they've got one heartbeat together as a team. There's always just three things I say: 'If anything goes bad, I did it. If anything goes semi-good, then we did it. If anything goes real good, they did it.' That's all it takes to get people to win."[2]

What makes a team a real team is the working together of each player on the field. Former head football coach, Bill McCartney worked hard to turn around the program at the University of Colorado, "I prayed daily that I could give this group of young men the leadership required to turn them into *a team,* instead of merely a group of talented individuals."[3] You each have the ability to play—you are on the team. But you may not play like a team. A team is more than a group of talented athletes. Your willingness to develop your ability and carry out your role on the team will affect how well you and your team does during the season. Coaches want the right players on the field for the right plays. And there has to be the right mix of talent on the field for the play to work. But this is not enough to create perfect chemistry—the ability to work as a single unit towards a common goal. You need every other player on the field and your coaches if you are going to learn to develop as a team.

After the passing of one of the University of Colorado's football quarterbacks, Coach McCartney noted the difficulty there was in achieving this unity as a team, "...you know, in coaching, you don't always have the perfect chemistry. You don't always have the bond you want. You're always reaching for it, both player and coach,..."[4] So how do we develop it? How do we get this team of talented people to function as a unit?

Motivated By A Common Focus

Teams that work well together have a common focus that moves them into action. Sometimes what brings together a team cannot be reproduced. Sometimes it is something that occurs quite unexpectedly.

At the end of the 1988 college football season the University of Colorado had finished its regular season with an 8-3 record. They went on to the Freedom Bowl and lost to Brigham Young. It was not the way they had wanted to end their season, but they had improved and were becoming a major force in college football. Although they finished the season ranked 25th in the Associated Press Poll they would begin the 1989 season in the top ten! During this year they would go undefeated 11-0 and claim the number one spot among college football teams. But what brought this team together was also what could have caused their demise. They watched their quarterback, Sal Aunese, die of cancer.

Early in the season as they beat Colorado State 45-20, something began to happen among the team members. Former coach

Bill McCartney notes, "Often, when one of our players would make an outstanding play, he'd point to Sal Aunese in a special seating section near the press box. The message was clear: *This is for you, Sal.*"[5] By the next game the entire team had the message. They together decided to dedicate the entire season to Sal! After the coin toss the entire team saluted Sal in his private box. He returned the salute, but this would be his last game in the stands. Only days later Sal was gone. What could have taken away the heart of the team now united it with new energy. Sal was not a quitter. His life brought the team together with renewed energy to give this season to him. Just days later the team beat Washington. And then the following game, at Missouri, the entire team kneeled and lifted one arm and pointed into the air towards heaven where Sal now resided. This season was for Sal.

The loss of a key player, a season committed to him, are not things you can create or plan on to bring the team together. But in 1989 it did for the University of Colorado.

Another unifying force can be good old school pride. For years the Notre Dame football team has united behind their alma mater. At a local high school in Cincinnati one team has begun a tradition in this area. In fact, their motto is "the tradition continues." This is another unifying force. It can be developed by coaches and players, as long as there is respect for the school. Although not as strong of a unifying force as the first example, this has been used with some success by college and high school teams.

Former University of Colorado coach Bill McCartney once inspired his team for one key game against Nebraska. He told each player to dedicate the game to someone. They had to then tell that person that they were playing that game for that individual. The strategy worked and they beat Nebraska that year!

However, the most powerful force that unites teams is not physical or earthly. It is spiritual. It is a unity that only God can develop. In 1984 I watched this focus unify the entire varsity football team at Council Rock High School in Newtown, Pennsylvania. We held Team Huddles for the team at one of the player's homes each week the day before the game. During that season 33 of the varsity players attended these huddles or chapels. Twelve already had a personal relationship with God. But by the end of the season all 33 had a relationship with Christ. Players would kneel in the end zone in prayer after touchdowns. They would pray throughout the game. They would come together after each win and thank Him. That team went on to win the league championship. Since that day I have watched other teams—professional, collegiate, and high school—unite around knowing God. The effect is always tremendous team unity.

Team unity or perfect chemistry on a team requires that the team have a common focus. If the only thing your team can rally around is your school then that is at least one thing. But there are much stronger unifying forces that can capture a team and bring about that single heartbeat that every player and coach seeks and hopes will develop early in the season.

Be A Team Player

If you are on the team, any athletic team, you are there because you like the sport, you want to improve at it, and you are willing to learn. If you want to play go out for the team! If you are on the team it is expected that you want to play.

A 1935 football game between Dartmouth and Princeton

took place in a blinding snow storm. Dartmouth had the ball. And as a Dartmouth player took off into the snow with the ball in hand there was no doubt that he was on his way to a touchdown. There was no Princeton Tiger within ten feet of him. However, on the sidelines, a spectator watching the player run down the field could hardly contain himself. He ran onto the field and made a perfect tackle. The tackle was nullified, a touchdown was awarded, and the spectator was tossed out of the stadium.[6]

A Team Player Plays By The Rules

Being a part of the team also means you will play by the rules. You are wanting the best for the team. That means you don't want what you do to hurt the team.

In 1929 during a college game between Washington and Oregon one of the coaches began yelling as he watched the opposing team's player running untouched for the end zone. "Who will stop him?" he cried out from the sidelines. And with that a sub player from off the bench yelled back , "I will coach." And he ran onto the field and made the tackle, but that was an illegal substitution!

If you are going to play you have to be on the team and in the game. But even if you come off the bench, the coach will expect you as well as the starters to be mentally and physically prepared.

A Team Player Is Always Alert On The Field

On April 26, 1931, in a baseball game between Washington and New York, Lyn Lary was rounding second base after Lou

Gehrig had sent the ball into center field. Lyn looked up to see the centerfielder catch the ball and assumed the inning was over and jogged off the field and into the dugout. Meanwhile, Lou Gehrig continued to run the bases. What he and the crowd had seen was the ball go out of the park for a home run and then bounce back into the playing field where it was caught by the outfielder. Lou circled the bases for his home run but was called out for passing Lyn Lary who had gone into the dugout!

Build Respect For Your Teammates And Coach

I believe that the reason we don't work well as a team can be traced to a lack of respect for our teammates or even our coaches. We don't see that each of our teammates can and do add an important and significant part to our team as a whole. Former UCLA head basketball coach John Wooden once said, "It's amazing how much can be accomplished if no one cares who gets the credit."[7] We need to become committed to seeing each athlete on our team become the best he can be. But to do this we need a correct and balanced view of our own abilities.

In a 1928 game between Notre Dame and Army Johnny O'Brien entered the game with the score tied 6 to 6. Everyone knew why he had been placed in the game. He stood six foot four and could reach over everyone to catch the ball. And that is just what he did. He caught the ball on the 15 and with a missed tackle by Army he easily got into the end zone. Immediately he was off the field and back on the bench. He was a one play specialist. He knew his role and carried it out flawlessly.

Do you know your strengths? In a court of law, a Notre Dame football star appeared as a witness in a civil suit.

The judge asked, "Are you a member of this year's Notre Dame football team?"

"Yes, Your Honor," the athlete replied.

"What position do you play?"

"I play center, Your Honor."

"How good a center are you?" the judge inquired.

"Sir," came the confident reply, "I'm the best center Notre Dame ever had."

The Notre Dame coach was in the court and was quite surprised by the reply. Though an excellent ballplayer, he always had seemed modest and unpretentious.

Later, he asked the player why he had said what he had.

"I didn't want to, coach, but there was no choice. I was under oath."[8]

Know your strengths and abilities. Don't sell yourself short, however. But also don't insist on your way. Work as a team.

Joe Paterno, head coach for Penn State, said in the book *Football My Way,* "If we could get that feeling—that 'we' and 'us' instead of 'I' and 'me'—so you can feel the love and respect for each other, they lose that individuality for the good of the team. When they lose themselves in something they think is a bit bigger than they are, they will be tough to beat."[9]

This sense of "teamness" or "perfect chemistry" takes place when the team has a common and shared focus, a respect for their teammates, and a respect for their coach. But to do this we need to lose ourselves in something bigger than us. There is only one focus that is above all others. There is only one coach who has no faults and is perfect in what He says and does. This coach is the only one who can give each of us a proper view of ourselves and our teammates. This is a coach we need to know better.

On the professional football field players and coaches seem to always be found huddling together and talking to God. Why? Because there is no other person who deserves our attention like Him. Our talent is from Him. The only lasting common focus for a team is from Him. He exhorts us to respect ourselves, our teammates, and our coaches. He brings about that "teamness" and "perfect chemistry" on the field and in life.

Father, thanks for making me as you have. Thank you for each of my teammates and their unique roles and abilities. Help me to encourage their development and skills for our team. Help me to fulfill my role and develop my skills. Thank you for our coaches. Make us a team that displays team unity on and off the field.

[1] Phyllis and Zander Hollander, Amazing But True Sports Stories (New York: Scholastic, Inc. , 1986), p. 69

[2] John C. Maxwell, Developing The Leader's Around You (Nashville: Thomas Nelson Publishers, 1995), p. 2.

[3] Bill McCartney with Dave Diles, From Ashes To Glory (Nashville: Thomas Nelson Publishers, 1990), p. 23.

[4] Ibid. p. 52.

[5] Ibid. pp. 46-47

[6] Paul Lee Tan, Encyclopedia Of 7700 Illustrations (Rockville, Maryland: Assurance Publishers, 1980), p. 1125.

[7] Craig Clifford and Randolph M. Feezell, Coaching for Character (Champaign, IL: Human Kinetics Publishers,Inc., 1997), p. 40.

[8] Rusty Wright and Linda Raney Wright, Secrets of Successful Humor (San Bernardino, CA: Here's Life Publishers, 1985), p. 128.

[9] John P. McCarthy, Coaching Youth Football - 2nd Edition (Cincinnati, OH: Better Way Books, 1995), p. 101.

TIME OUT
Designed By God

1. According to Psalm 139:13-16, who designed you both physically and spiritually?

    How does David, the writer of Psalm 139, evaluate the finished product? (v. 14)

    Take a minute and thank God for how He has made you.

2. If you know Christ personally, what is true about you based upon these verses:

    > I Cor. 6:19-20
    > I Peter 4:10-11
    > Eph. 4:15,16

3. We are God's people, we have gifts from Him, we are to use them for the benefit of others. Look at Phil. 2:5-16. List some of the things that are found here that would be important to think about and act upon as a believer with the right focus and heartbeat.

    Take a few minutes and go back over these items and ask God to begin to make these things true in your life. Then thank Him for doing it.

10

Confidence Builders

Georgia Tech's star fullback, Canty Alexander, was taking a beating from a tough opponent one Saturday afternoon. It was late in the second half, with Georgia Tech down by five touchdowns, all hope of victory was now gone, and it became a game of survival.

"With a few minutes left to play Georgia Tech players went into a huddle. The quarterback called a play that would send fullback Canty Alexander over center.

'Don't run that one,' pleaded the weary fullback, 'Last time we tried it, they almost twisted my neck off.'

'All right,' snapped the quarterback, 'We'll send the left half around right end.'

'Oh, no,' begged the left halfback, 'don't do that. The last time we tried that play their end nearly broke my leg.'

'Okay, then,' snapped the soft-hearted quarterback, 'Then let's try the right half around left end.'

'No, you don't,' piped up the right halfback, 'Last time we ran that play they almost caved in a couple of my ribs.'

'Well, boys, what'll we do?' asked the befuddled Georgia Tech quarterback.

'I know what we should do,' spoke up a guard, 'let's throw a long incomplete forward pass.'"[1]

The Power of Fear

Fear is a powerful motivating force. It can either give you the energy to compete at a higher level or cause you to run and hide. When your body senses fear your whole body is moved into action. Adrenaline is released by your body and you are prepared for action. Now you have a choice. Stay and act or turn and flee.

How you handle fear will make or break you. Standing at 6 foot 8 inches, weighing 280 pounds you would not think that former football player John Matuszak was affected by fear. In public he was seen as a "havoc-wreaking, heavy-drinking, hard-hitting player who was as much of a threat off the field as on." However, his friends knew he was simply a "280 pound puppy dog just begging to be stroked."

John was ridiculed as a young boy for his "gawky, beanpole appearance." He had two brothers, but both died of cystic fibrosis. He tried to hide his true feelings and fears with alcohol and drugs only to die at the early age of 38 from a massive heart attack. "According to Los Angeles Times writer Mark Heisler, John Matuszak was 'beset by fears he couldn't acknowledge.'"[2]

Let Fear Work For You

There will always be times that you will find yourself in competition with someone bigger, stronger, or more skilled than you are. When that happens you need to let fear work for you.

Back in September of 1995 just before the San Francisco 49ers met the New England Patriots, Jerry Rice revealed one of the keys to his total athletic performance. What was it? It was focusing on failure. That's right. "Failure scares me and keeps me focused. I won't go into a game saying, 'We've got this won.' If you feel that way, you relax. When you relax, you drop footballs." [3]

Being a competitor can cause sleeplessness the night before the game. But Jerry uses these times to his advantage. When he wakes up at 4 am he takes time to review the game in his head. This is when he gets mentally prepared. And if he has a knot in his stomach he knows he is fine. He says, "Butterflies tell me the fire is still inside."[4]

Be Courageous

It has been said that courage is not the absence of fear but the mastery of it. It is also believed that about 90% of our ailments begin with the fear of something. How can we master our fears? How can we not be crippled by them? The answer is in the true story of a teenager who lived thousands of years ago.

During these times there were often battles between different groups of people. In one battle it was decided that rather than have all the warriors fight, each group would pick their best warrior and they would meet each other alone on the battlefield. For days the one side presented their man. A nine-foot-six tall man fully clothed in armor. The other side had no reply. It was at that time that a brother of some of the warriors showed up at the camp. He had been sent to deliver food to them but as he arrived the giant of a man again stood in the valley taunting the people. Surprised that not one of his brothers or the other warriors were willing to stand against him, he was impressed to go into the battle himself. Although only a shepherd and still a teenager, he attempted to prepare by using one of the other warriors' armor. But that was not working well. He made the decision to go into the battle with only his sling shot and his normal clothes. He not only took his opponent off guard but struck him with his first stone and after he fell to the ground he severed his head with the giant's own sword. His name was David.

What was the real secret of David's success while the others cowered in fear? It was who he knew. He knew the one who was greater than all of the people doing battle. David did not fear death. He knew the one who made him. He knew what happened after this life? He found strength in Him. Have you discovered this person? Do you experience His strength? Do you have confidence that there is life after this life? You can.

Father, I want to know you and the power that you can give to make me courageous.

[1] Bill Stern, Bill Stern's Favorite Football Stories (New York: Doubleday and Company, Inc. 1948), pp. 14,15.

[2] Our Daily Bread, (Sept.,Oct.,Nov. 1991), Thursday, Sept. 5,1991.

[3] Jeffrey Zaslow, "Jerry Rice - Fear is good," USA Weekend, (Sept. 15-17, 1995), p. 22.

[4] Ibid.

TIME OUT
Spiritual Confidence

Do you know that you can know for certain where you will spend eternity? You can! God's Word assures us of this truth and we can trust God at His Word.

1. Look at John 10:27-30. Think about each of these questions and use this passage of scripture to answer them.

   a. Who is talking in this passage?

   b. Who are the sheep that Jesus refers to?

   c. What relationship do these people have with Jesus?

   d. What has Jesus given to these people?

   e. Will they ever perish? Never?

   f. These people know God and will never perish. We can be sure that this is true because: (find the verse that goes with the statements below)

   1) Verse _____ says that no one shall snatch them out of the hand of Jesus—We are in His hand.

2) Verse _____ says that no one is able to snatch them out of the Father's hand—We are in His hand too. God's strength and power is greater than man's and we cannot lose what God assures us that we do indeed have and that is eternal life.

2. In I John 5:11 what does it say that a believer actually has?

3. If we don't have the Son of God in our lives—we are not a believer—then we cannot have eternal life. But if we do have Him then we must have eternal life according to I John 5:11,12. So according to I John 5:13 what are we to know that we have?

4. Who, according to these passages, is responsible to make sure we receive eternal life as believers in Christ?
    a. Romans 8:28-30

    b. Philippians 1:6

5. You can trust God at His Word to do what He says. As a believer you should also notice that God is working in and through you and this will give you greater assurance that you are His child. Note these truths in the verses below and record what should be true of you as you walk with God:

    a. Romans 8:15
    b. I John 2:3-6
    c. I John 5:1-3

Realize that as a believer you are not perfect yet. That is why God makes provision for our failures (I John 2:1,2). While we do not continue to sin when we walk with Him it is possible that a true believer will fail. But just like a student who trips in a hallway at school and decides to get up quickly and start walking again, a believer who sins should quickly confess any known sin and continue to walk in fellowship with God. It would be silly for a student after he falls to decide not to walk any more and resort to crawling; in the same way it would be inappropriate for a believer who sins to continue in it. Remember, sin in a believer's life breaks fellowship with God but does not change the fact that he is a member of the family of God. You can be sure that you have eternal life! Take a minute and thank God that He has given you eternal life. If you don't yet know Him why not ask Him into your life today?

11

Communication: The Key to Victory

Sometimes how a sport develops can best illustrate a key to how it is best played. This is in part the case for the game of football. Back in October, 1895, in Atlanta, Georgia, the University of Georgia was playing the University of North Carolina. The game was played hard by both sides and with only five minutes left to play the score was still deadlocked at nothing to nothing.

North Carolina had possession at their own 40-yard line. When the ball was snapped Carolina's left halfback took it. He placed it under his arm and headed out towards the goal line. Running interference for him was George Butler, Carolina's quarterback.

The North Carolina runner had not gone far when Georgia broke through and had the Carolina halfback trapped. In the midst of all the noise and activity a voice called out to the trapped runner. It was the voice of the team captain and quarterback, George Butler. With a sharp command he yelled, "Let me have the ball!" The only problem was that the quarterback was at least six yards ahead of him. But the halfback instantly responded and threw the ball into George's waiting arms. George then took off towards the goal line for a seventy yard touchdown. While the crowd sat in amazement, the players and referees were trying to sort out what had just happened. And when they let the touchdown stand North Carolina had defeated Georgia by a score of 6 to nothing by using football's first forward pass—the result of quick communication between two players on the same team.[1]

Know When To Talk, And Always Listen

Communication in sports needs to be specific and needs to include as few or as many players as it will take to carry off the play. In football, the no-huddle offense can create some very poor play on the field if the entire team does not understand when the snap will occur or what the play will be. On the soccer field players with their back to the opposition can easily be taken advantage of if the other teammates do not notice a halfback or full-back coming up from behind and warn the player with the ball that a man is on him! In the same way, a team that doesn't talk on the soccer field when they have the ball will cause some of their players to kick the ball away too soon when that player really had plenty of time to dribble with the ball and set-up a play. Why? If the players never talk then they assume that they are on their own and can't tell if they have time or they don't have time. A team that talks will give players with the ball confidence that they have time to set up a play if they are use to hearing their teammates tell them of approaching opposing players!

Communication is key between players, coaches and players, and coaches and other coaches. No wonder we need all that head gear on the sidelines for football games! There is even electronics in quarterback's helmets today. The coaches in the sky boxes need to let the coach on the line know what the other team's defense and offense are doing. The coach on the sidelines needs to get key plays into the huddle on time so they can be called by the quarterback and then each player needs to fulfill his role at the right time when the ball is snapped for the play to accomplish what it was sent in to do. All this depends upon clear and specific communication.

In the 1952 Pro Bowl Blanton Collier, a former assistant and head coach for the Cleveland Browns was coaching the defense against a talented quarterback named Norm Van Brocklin. Blanton had seen this guy throw a seventy yard pass in order for the LA Rams to clench an NFL championship in 1951 against the Browns. Because of this he instructed his safeties in the Pro Bowl and especially Emlen Tunnell, "When Dutch comes into the game, you go back farther than you think he can throw it, then go back another twenty yards because, believe me, he'll throw it that far." So when Van Brocklin came into the game guess what happened? The safety Emlen got beat for a touchdown. Emlen came off the field, picked up the field phone, and said to the coach, "So help me, I'll never disbelieve you again in my life."[2]

Know Who's Talking To You

When your coach speaks you should listen carefully. But there are others who will try to talk to you on the field of play who should not be listened to!

Years ago in a football game between Duke and Pitt an unusual turnover occurred due to communication on the field. George McAfee, playing for Duke had just broken into the clear with the ball when he heard a voice behind him yell this command, "Let me have it, George!" Without looking, George tossed the ball backward right into the hands of a Pitt player who ran it down to Duke's ten-yard line and then scored on the next play.[3] The Pitt player had been the one who had commanded George to give him the ball.

Knowing who is talking to you can make or break you in the game. While a voice may sound friendly it may be an attempt to deceive you.

Know What To Say, And What Not To Say

Reggie White, perhaps the greatest defensive lineman to play the game of football, often was around guys on and off the field who would use language that would offend anyone with an ounce of character. While playing head-to-head against other linemen there was always opportunity for some one-on-one well chosen words between opposing players. During one pre-season game with Indianapolis Reggie was only playing on the field goal unit until a Colt lineman cursed at him. With that Reggie went to Buddy, his Philadelphia coach, and asked if he could play. Buddy sent him in for one play but the defense they were using caused Reggie to line up on the tight end instead of the tackle who had cursed at him. Since he couldn't talk to him during the play he ran up to him and said, "Don't you ever in your life use profanity on a man of God again." The Colt tackle then responded, "Reggie, I apologize. The guys on the sideline told me that you are a minister, and I'm sorry."[4]

In another situation, a Detroit rookie used foul language on him and Reggie simply stated to him, "Jesus is coming back soon, and I hope you're ready." This didn't stop the rookie's cursing at him and that just made Reggie all the more determined. He then yelled back across the field, "Jesus is coming back soon, and I hope you're ready." When they each broke from their huddles they lined up just a few inches from each other. Reggie said, "Jesus is coming back soon, and I don't think you're ready." Then at the snap of the ball Reggie said, "Here comes Jesus!" and he moved the rookie five yards back and he landed on the turf just in time to see Reggie sack his quarterback.

We need to be men of our word but we also need to choose our words carefully. There are more words in our language than curse words. And we can certainly learn to use them instead.

Talk And Listen To The Right Person

If you want to know the play, talk to the coach. If you make an adjustment to your route, let the quarterback know. If you want the defensive line to shift over a man and it's your job to call the plays, do it. If you want answers to a classroom subject, ask your teacher. If you need help developing your physical abilities and strength, ask your coach. If you want to begin and develop the spiritual dimension of your life then talk with your Creator.

Reggie understood the value and priority of talking to Him. In Reggie White's book, *God's Play Book*, he says, "God wants us to communicate with Him because He has a great plan for our lives."[5] When was the last time you talked with Him?

Father, I come to you. Help me see what you want me to see. Help me to hear what you want me to hear. Help me to do what you want me to do.

[1] Bill Stern, <u>Bill Stern's Favorite Football Stories</u> (New York: Doubleday and Company, Inc., 1950), pp. 12-13

[2] Jack Clary, <u>Pro Football's Great Moments</u> (New York: Bonanza Books, 1987), pp. 30-31.

[3] Bill Stern, <u>Bill Stern's Favorite Football Stories</u> (New York: Doubleday and Company, Inc., 1950), pp. 143-144.

[4] Reggie White, <u>God's Play Book</u> (Nashville: Thomas Nelson Publishers, 1998), p. 93.

[5] <u>Ibid</u>. p. 23.

TIME OUT
Communicating With God

God talks to us through His Word and we talk to God
through prayer.

1. From Psalm 1:1-3 why is it important to spend time in
    God's Word?

2. Talking with God in prayer is us coming to Him, embrac-
    ing His heart, and seeking to do His work in His strength.
    But before we get to that state of mind we may have some
    things to talk to God about. God wants us to come to
    Him honestly and openly. What are the things that you
    desire to bring before God at this time?

3. Spend some time talking to Him about these things. Ask
    Him to give you His heart towards them. Trust Him with
    them. Note in the following passages what God will do as
    we bring our requests to Him:

    a. Phil. 4:6,7

    b. Jeremiah 33:3

    c. Matt. 21: 21,22

    d. James 4:1-3

    e. John 14:13

4. According to Phil. 2:13, who is working in you?
   What is he doing?

5. How can we know that God will answer our prayers?
   (Look at the passages below to answer this question.)

    a. John 15:7

    b. John 14:14

    c. James 1:6-8

    d. Romans 8:26,27

    e. Romans 8:34

    Spend time thanking Him that: (1) He intercedes for you,
    (2) He is working in you to want and do His will, and
    (3) that He will answer you when you talk to Him.

12

Choose the Path to Victory

It was our first cold night of the football season. But the game did not make us think about the dropping temperatures. On Friday, September 22, 1995 the Harrison Wildcats were in a battle with the Anderson Redskins. Two teams with 2-1 records and this was a must win game to keep any chance of post-season play alive for either team.

With the game winding down to the final plays the Wildcats were trailing 23-21. An on-sides kick-off was attempted by the Wildcats and they managed to recover the ball. That set-up the opportunity for an amazing finale to this exciting game.

As the Wildcats moved down the field the Redskins defense played tough. They were able to get close to field goal range but it was third down. During their final time-out their field goal kicker could be seen sitting on the ground changing his shoe on his kicking foot in hopes of having enough time left to get into the game and kick the winning field goal for his team, but that would not occur.

After moving the ball closer to the goal the Wildcats were met with a fourth down, no time outs remaining, and the crowd was chanting in unison as the final 10 seconds of the game were running out. Quarterback Nick Elrod glanced to the sidelines to see what the coach wanted to do. The Redskins had kept their pass receiver from running out of bounds after his catch and the Wildcats had no time to get a field goal attempt set-up.

As the ball was hiked the Redskins converged upon the quarterback and flattened him well behind the line of scrimmage. He had been looking down the field at a receiver running to the end zone on the left side of the field. But as he was about to begin moving his arm forward to pass to him he was hit by two Redskins and fumbled the ball as time ran out. Thinking that the game was over and the final score was 23-21 the entire Redskin team ran onto the field to celebrate the victory. Even the defensive players began moving towards the large group of over 100 players and coaches jumping on each other on the field.

But little noticed, except by those in the stands, this game was not over. The ball was still alive. And that was when tailback B.J. Holbert picked up the loose ball. The Redskins paid no attention to his wrestling with the pigskin and looking down the field to his open receiver in the end zone. As the referee caught the action he moved down the field to watch the results of the Wildcat player's pass to the end zone. He tossed it as hard as he could and in order to catch the ball the receiver came out of the end zone to about the five yard line, caught the ball, and then fixed his eyes on the referee as he gently in almost a questioning frolic moved into the end zone. Immediately the referee signaled that it was indeed a touchdown. At this point the Redskins became aware of their mistake. They could argue and respond in shock. But the score was 27-23 with the Wildcats pulling off a big upset on the Anderson Redskins with no time remaining. The extra kick was not attempted. The game was over.

One of the most meaningless stats is a half-time score. In the

Anderson vs. Harrison game Anderson was ahead 13 to 7 at the half. But that meant nothing in terms of how the game turned out. From the Harrison perspective this was a lesson on how to rescue victory from the jaws of defeat. From the Anderson point of view it was how to grab defeat from the jaws of victory. What may look like a win may not be one. What may look like certain defeat is not necessarily the case.

It has been said that, "Winning is a habit. Unfortunately, so is losing."[1] There are some amazing single game records that have been recorded over the years. But besides winning big in a game consider also their season records. Haven (Kansas) High beat Sylvia High in 1928 by the score of 256 to nothing. During their entire season they beat their opponents by a combined score of 578 to nothing. In 1973, Arthur Hill High School in Saginaw, Michigan, outscored its nine opponents by the combined score of 443 to nothing. Certainly you would have rather been on the winning side in these contests than the losing one. Victory is a choice. Unfortunately, so is losing.

In 1977 the MacAlester College Scots lost all eight of their football games by a total of 532 to 39. Some of their defeats were 62 to 7, 46 to 0, 51 to 7, and 55 to 13. They had players on their team who had played for four full seasons and never taken a half-time lead into the locker room. Things had become so bad that in one game the team went into the huddle and the coach thought that they would never come out! To twist coach Vince Lombardi's philosophy, "To them losing wasn't everything; it was the only thing." Things were so bad that there was talk of dropping the entire football program at the school. And on October 28, 1978 they lost their 40th straight game setting the NCAA record for most straight defeats. On that day the longest run in the game occurred when the campus dog ran onto the field; it was also the play that brought the biggest cheer from the crowd. They had lost 44 to 0. But there was cause for some excitement in this score. The year before they had lost to the same team 70 to 0. It was clear that their defense was improving. Finally, on Sept. 6, 1980 with the score tied 14 to 14 with Mt. Scenario College of Lady Smith, Wisconsin, they kicked a field goal with 11 seconds left in the game to win the game and end their now 50 game losing streak.

When Reggie White went to play for the Green Bay Packers in 1993 the team had not been in a Championship game since the days of Vince Lombardi in 1968. Although the team's record had improved and they were having winning seasons, they had become content to lose. Reggie had not come to Green Bay to lose and he let his teammates know it in no uncertain terms. Then in 1995 Green Bay had to go to San Francisco to play the 49ers—defending champions and winners of five Super Bowls in fourteen years. Could the Packers beat them? They didn't even know if they could do it. Being the defensive leader on the team there was a need to give the guys some incentive to play hard on defense. When he had been in Philly there was a smash-for-cash program where they would give out $100 for every big play—a sack, interception, fumble, touchdown, or big hit. It seemed to work for even the guys making millions. So they ran the program in Green Bay too. By the end of the season their fund was running out. So to keep things going Reggie and Sean Jones put in some of their own money to keep it going. Perhaps that was a factor in the Packers' upset of the 49ers by a score of 27 to 17. Reggie certainly was affected by it. He had to pay out to his teammates $9,000 of his $13,000 game check! There were that many good plays during that one game![2]

Former Dallas Cowboys coach Tom Landry made this statement on October 7, 1990: "I know how to lose a game without losing the will to win or my dignity." He went on to say, "What is first in my life is my faith, family and the game I love." Do you know how to keep striving to win in the face of defeat? You need to stay on the path to victory.

We all want to make it to the winner's circle. We all want to experience the joy of victory. In the most popular best selling book of all time, victory is described as hearing these specific words from one's own master: "Well done good and faithful servant, enter into the joy of your master." (Matthew 25:21) In another place it is said that faith is our victory. (I John 5:4) The path to victory begins in the hearts and minds of the athlete first and involves the athlete's relationship with God.

If you are going to choose the path to victory you need to have a definition that will work for both a team and an individual. You can choose the path to victory by 1. being faithful to pursue what you are called to do to the very end 2. with a good heart by faith in the living God keep moving ahead and 3. leaving the results to God. This definition will work for an individual as well as a team.

Be Faithful To Pursue What You Are Called To Do To The Very End

Some years ago when Tim Krumrie was playing for the Cincinnati Bengals in a game against Denver, time was nearly gone with the Bengals trailing by four touchdowns but you wouldn't have known it by looking at Tim. To him a 14 to 42 deficit is no different than a 0 to 0 tie. He was not drafted until the ninth round back in 1983. "I was too short, too slow, too light," Tim says. But all the talk was disproved by his heart. His desire, determination, and dedication made up for it all. Former coach Sam Wyche said, "He made it in the league by being an over-achiever, by working harder than the next guy. We need some more of that, no question. That needs to spread around a little more." Tim says, "Hopefully, it's a disease and it'll catch on with other players. Just because you're out of a ball game doesn't mean you have to quit." "No matter what the score is, you still go 100%. I hope, watching me, no matter what the score is, other players will go 100% all the time."

If you simply follow the first part of this definition you will experience some success. But you have to put it together with the second part if you want to choose the path to victory with unseen and surprising power for the game and life itself.

On January 3, 1993 the Buffalo Bills were playing the Houston Oilers. Frank Reich had stepped up to the challenge of being the Bills quarterback with their starter out. In the second half Frank threw four touchdown passes erasing a 35 to 3 deficit. Although the Bills were now ahead 38 to 35 Houston was able to tie the game to send it into overtime. Buffalo then won the game in overtime with a field goal. Afterwards Frank was asked about the game, one of the greatest comebacks in NFL history, and his first words were, "I thank Jesus for the strength..."

With A Good Heart By Faith In The Living God Keep Moving Ahead

Living with a good heart is one that is not lifted up in pride but is focused upon being a servant. Frank recognized this as he brought the Bills back from certain defeat. He knew he was simply a tool in the hand of God. And he thanked Him for the strength to carry out what he was called to do.

Think back to my first illustration. Could it be that the Harrison Wildcats who defeated the Anderson Redskins had this unseen victor on the field with them or is it simply a case of pride going before the fall. The talk at Anderson all week before the game was that the Wildcats were no threat to them. It sounded as if the game would be a romp. But it turned into a seesaw battle with final second heroics. God humbles the proud. But it is better to learn humility now rather than spend life without God and go into eternity apart from His presence. If this can be used to bring more players to Himself then that is far better than beating an infinite number of teams which only bring temporary happiness and success.

The historical meeting of David and Goliath also serves to demonstrate the priority of a good hearted person living by faith in God. Goliath with all his size and ability with a great defense and offense is faced with a small young boy with no visible defense and only a seemingly insignificant offensive weapon. But behind him stood this unseen power which was far greater than all the Goliaths that could be found. When he stood before the nearly ten foot tall man dressed in armor and simply approached him with a sling shot and some pebbles in hand it looked like a classic mismatch. But Goliath did not know David's source of strength. And because of David's servant heart and willingness and desire to be His tool in the battle the victory would be his. David chose the path to victory by trusting in God Himself. He used what God had trained him to do and rested in His power for the victory.

Leave The Results To God

One of the greatest fourth quarter comebacks occurred on

November 8, 1987 when Neil Lomax led the Cardinals to victory. St. Louis was down 3 to 28 to Tampa Bay at the beginning of the fourth quarter.

Just two minutes and 18 seconds into the final quarter, Neil found Robert Awalt to complete a 4-yard scoring pass. One minute and three seconds later, a James Wilder fumble was recovered by Cardinal linebacker Niko Noga and returned for a 23-yard touchdown. It was now 17 to 28.

The defense held and the Cardinals were able to score again in less than four minutes on an eleven yard pass from Neil to J.T. Smith. It was now 24 to 28. With only 61 seconds left in the game, Neil hit Smith again with a 17-yard pass for a 31 to 28 victory.

From Neil's days playing football at Portland State University in Portland, Oregon he found strength for the game in his relationship with God. When we choose the path to victory, we leave the scoreboard in His hands.

It is easy to see why athletes find strength in the living God when you consider what he did for the world. What may seem like a strange way to reach victory is actually the most triumphant and powerful path to victory.

Nearly two thousand years ago one man did what no other could. He gave His life for all men. Jesus came to earth to fulfill a plan set down before the beginning of time. He would die on a cross. First, He encountered a mock trial with trumped up charges but did not seek to counter them. A crown of thorns was pressed into His head. Then He received 40 lashes. This was accomplished by a leather whip with either glass or rock embedded in it being whipped onto His shoulders and with a quick jerk ripped down His back. The effect of this would be to tear the skin apart. By the end you could have moved the torn tissues apart and seen the internal organs. In this condition Jesus then carried His cross for His own crucifixion.

At the site of His crucifixion He was either nailed to the cross with one nail in each hand and one through His two feet and then lifted up and dropped into the hole in the ground. Or, He was nailed to the cross bar and then lifted up and dropped into the vertical part of the cross already in the ground and then His feet were nailed to it. But whichever occurred the effect would be the same, His shoulders would have dislocated upon impact. This made it necessary for Him to lift himself up to breathe. He would do this by pushing up on His nailed feet and taking a breath. He would have to do this each time to keep alive on the cross. Jesus endured the cross to the end and left the results to God. And on the third day He rose from the dead. Jesus lives today. You can know His strength and power as you accept Him and live for Him.

Consider this day whom you will follow. Why not choose life over temporary and passing excitement? Why not choose the path to victory in life as well as your sport?

Father, thank You for providing the path to victory for me through your Son. Help me live my life for Him and do it in His strength.

[1] Reggie White, God's Play Book (Nashville: Thomas Nelson Publishers, 1998), p. 13.

[2] Ibid. pp. 13-15.

TIME OUT
Living By Faith

1. The truly victorious person lives by faith in God. What do these passages say about that?
   a. Heb. 11:6
   b. Heb. 11:32-34

2. In light of this, how are we to live now according to Heb. 12:1-3?

3. What does God want us to do in this world?
   a. Acts 1:8   b. Matt. 28:18-20   c. 2 Cor. 5:20

4. God wants to use you to tell others about Him. What did the Apostle Paul do in Romans 10:1?

   What should we do for those who need to know Christ? Since we should pray for the salvation of others why not begin now to pray for those you know who need Christ. Make a list below and begin to pray daily for them.

5. Learn to share your faith by reading the material in the Appendix Six on how to share your faith in God. Choose the path to victory and help others find the path, too. Read Appendix Three (For additional Time Outs turn to Appendix Two.)

Commencement

If you have just completed these Huddles and their Time Outs you have just begun your spiritual journey. There is so much more and you have only tasted the tip of the iceberg of all that God has for you and wants to do through you.

Keep practicing the truths you have learned. Think about teaching them to others. There are several appendices that are included here to help you do this. Your teammates and friends are just waiting for someone like you to lead them on the path to victory. Ask God how He would like for you to proceed and then trust Him to give you the strength to do it.

If you would like more help on how to impact your friends for Christ check out www.gocampus.org or call 1-877-GOCAMPUS.

Enjoy the adventure. It has just begun!

1

Starting An Eternal Relationship

God loves you and He wants you to know Him personally! Are you ready to meet Him? John 3:16 says, "For God so loved the world, that He gave His only begotten Son, that whoever believes in Him should not perish, but have eternal life." God has made it possible for you to know Him personally by sending His Son into the world. He offers eternal life to you. John 17:3 says, "And this is eternal life, that they may know Thee, the only true God, and Jesus Christ whom Thou hast sent." A relationship with God is one that lasts forever. Are you interested?

You may be thinking, "Why doesn't everyone have an eternal relationship with God?" It is because of sin. Romans 3:23 says, "for all have sinned and fall short of the glory of God." And in Romans 6:23 it says, "For the wages of sin is death, but the free gift of God is eternal life in Christ Jesus our Lord." Sin was used in the game of archery. It described the distance between where the arrow should go and where it actually fell. In terms of our relationship with God it describes His holy character and our inability to achieve that mark. We always are short of perfection.

But since we all deserve death, God made it possible for sin to be paid for by the death of His Son, Jesus Christ. Romans 5:8

says, "But God demonstrates His own love toward us, in that while we were yet sinners, Christ died for us." Although Jesus did die for us, He is no longer dead. In fact He lives so we might now have life in Him. I Corinthians 15:3-6 says, "For I delivered to you as of first importance what I also received, that Christ died for our sins according to the Scriptures, and that He was buried, and that He was raised on the third day according to the Scriptures, and that He appeared to Cephas (Peter), then to the twelve. After that He appeared to more than five hundred brethren at one time, most of whom remain until now, but some have fallen asleep;..."

Jesus is the only way to know God personally. In John 14:6, "Jesus said to him, 'I am the way, and the truth, and the life; no one comes to the Father, but through Me." The free gift of God is eternal life through Jesus Christ His Son. But before the gift is yours you must receive it. Romans 10:13 says, "Whoever will call upon the name of the Lord will be saved." And in Revelation 3:20 Jesus says, "Behold, I stand at the door and knock; if anyone hears My voice and opens the door, I will come in to him, and will dine with him, and he with Me."

If you would like to begin an eternal relationship with God you can do so right now. Simply turn from self to God. Trust Jesus Christ to come into your life, forgive your sins, and make you the person He created you to be. Remember, like any gift, it is not yours until you decide by an act of your will to accept it. You can accept Jesus Christ right now by simply telling God what you would like to do. Here is a brief prayer that may help you express what you feel towards God.

Jesus, thank you for dying on the cross for my sin. I ask you to come into my life, forgive my sin, and make me the person you created me to be. Thank you for giving me eternal life. Amen.

If you meant these words as you said them to God then He came into your life and you began an eternal relationship with God. You now have begun the greatest adventure of all time. So what do you do now? Here are a few suggestions:

First, if you haven't completed the Team Huddles yet make sure you look at Team Huddle Ten. It will help you know for sure that you have begun an eternal relationship with God. If you have already seen that Huddle take some time to review the Time Out in that lesson. Second, complete the Team Huddles you have not yet done and the suggested appendices that are mentioned in each one. You have made the most important decision of your life when you asked Jesus Christ into your life! You have begun a most incredible journey that will last for eternity.

A Note To Those Who Have Not Yet Made This Decision

If you are still thinking about making this decision for Christ but haven't yet, continue to read through the Team Huddles and visit one of our websites like: www.beyondextreme.com There will be a time when you will want to receive Christ.

2

Developing an Eternal Relationship with God

If you have begun an eternal relationship with God you will want to continue to develop it. The Team Huddles have several huddles that focus upon how to do this. But remember that it is a relationship. It will take time. You will get to know some basic things about God right at the beginning. If you complete all the Time Outs in this book you will have covered the basics. But that is only the beginning.

You need to continue to get to know God. God will lead you to other believers to spend time with and even a good church. God has brought you into His family and there are many others who know Him. He has also designed the body of Christ so that each believer is vitally important to one another. You will grow as you spend time with God and others who bring you to the truth of God's Word. This includes both the example of living in the truth and teaching what it says. You should find that both what a person says is true from the Bible is also exactly how they live. These are the ones to spend time with as they will help you grow up in your relationship with God.

But remember, no one is perfect in this life. We all make mistakes even as believers. So grant others the grace to fail, but encourage them to confess their mistakes and move on. Then learn to walk in dependence upon God's power to live the Christian life. Here is a brief study on this topic for you to do on your own. Also, if you are doing the Team Huddles as a daily devotional then this should be a lesson that you do as a Time Out probably after you have done the other twelve Time Outs in the book. After this Time Out I have listed 18 more passages to look at along with a key question so you will have enough Time Outs to make your devotional use of this book last for 31 days in all.

TIME OUT

Walk in Dependence Upon God

1. What does Eph. 5:1,2 say we should do?

2. From Rom. 12:1,2 what must occur in our lives if we are to be imitators of God and walk in love?

3. Should we confess known sin (I John 1:9)? Why?

4. According to Eph. 5:15,16 what should we do and be aware of?

5. From Eph. 5:17 what should we seek to understand? Where do we discover God's will?

6. Where does the power come from to want to do and to be able to do God's will? (Look back at Phil. 2:13)

7. Who do we depend upon to do God's will and Word? (Eph. 5:18)

8. How will we know we are filled with His Spirit and doing His will?

Specifically: we will be able to do God's Word in His power and what we confessed we failed at in our own strength we will now be able to do in His strength.. Generally: we will experience the results of obedience to His will as found in Eph. 5:19-21. Make a list of the results from Eph. 5:19-21:

9. Based upon Gal. 2:20 what part does faith have in walking with God?

By faith ask God to reveal to you anything that is displeasing to Him. Don't argue or rationalize away what He says to you. Agree with God. Confess it to Him. Then ask Him to fill you with His Holy Spirit. Now trust Him to enable you to do what you just confessed you could not do or failed to do. Also, trust Him to enable you to do His word as you learn it in the Bible. This is the life of faith. This is what makes it so exciting and a great adventure. When God works though your life in a way that can only be described as supernatural you will discover one of the joys of your new relationship with God.

Time Outs 14-31

In each of the following Time Outs take a minute to ask God to speak to you today. Then look up the Bible verses and write down in a notebook what you discover that the passage says about God and what it says about Man. Then consider the question found under the passage for that Time Out. Finally, take time to ask God to do in your life what you discovered from the passage and then pray for others you know who need to learn and practice what you discovered from the passage. This should take no more than 10 minutes in all. However, the more you spend time with God the faster the time will go by. So don't be surprised if you discover you are spending 12, 15, or 30 minutes with God each day. Here are additional Time Outs for you to use as daily devotions:

Time Out 14
Hebrews 11:1-6 – Why is it important to live by faith?

Time Out 15
Hebrews 11:7-12 – Is it easy to live by faith? Why or why not?

Time Out 16
Hebrews 11:13-16 – What do men and women of faith look forward to?

Time Out 17
Hebrews 11:17-31 – Is the life of faith challenging? Why or why not?

Time Out 18
Hebrews 11:32-40 – What are some amazing things that believers have done by faith?

Time Out 19
Hebrews 12:1-3 – Who should we focus upon to keep living by faith?

Time Out 20
Hebrews 12:4-11 – What is the purpose of discipline? What does it prove about who we really are?
Time Out 21
Hebrews 12:12-17 – What role does discipline have in the life of faith?

Time Out 22
Hebrews 12:18-24 – What type of kingdom have we become a resident of?

Time Out 23
Hebrews 12:25-29 – What confidence do we have that others don't have?

Time Out 24
Ephesians 1:1-14 – How many spiritual blessings has God given to us? Of the ones mentioned which one do you find most important to you now?

Time Out 25
Ephesians 1:15-23 – What did the writer (Paul) pray for?

Time Out 26
Ephesians 2:1-10 – How is your life different now from what it was like? What has happened that has made it different? What should now be true of your life?

Time Out 27

Ephesians 2:11-22 – How is your new family relationship different from your old family relationship?

Time Out 28

Ephesians 3:1-13 – Mercy is not getting what you deserve. Grace is getting what you don't deserve. How was God's grace shown in Paul's life? (Note: Paul is the writer of the book of Ephesians.)

Time Out 29

Ephesians 3:14-21 – What does the writer (Paul) pray for his readers?

Time Out 30

Ephesians 4:1-16 – What has God provided us with so we can grow more stable in our faith?

Time Out 31

Ephesians 4:17-32 – How should you live your new life in Christ? What area do you need God to work on in your life the most? How could you learn to do this area by faith?

You may want to continue going through the book of Ephesians a paragraph at a time in your daily devotions. When you finish you may want to go paragraph by paragraph through the book of I Thessalonians, then the book of Romans, then the book of Psalms.

For more information on growing as a believer contact Student Venture at 100 Lake Hart Dr., Orlando, FL 32832 or www.studentventure.com on the web.

3

Using Team Huddles as an Outreach Tool

Students and adults have made use of this tool to reach students for Christ in their cities. You can too. This is a simple tool that will increase the spiritual interest among students and bring them to an opportunity to begin an eternal relationship with God.

Using Team Huddles As A Salting Tool

Each of the Huddles is designed to focus students on their need to develop the spiritual area of their lives. Students who have heard many of these talks, some over and over again, for four entire sport seasons have been brought closer to considering their need for God if not finally reaching the point where they actually do decide to respond and accept Jesus Christ as their Savior and Lord.

If there is a lack of spiritual hunger for God among your students you might want to offer to a coach of one sport these Team Huddle talks. Simply ask the coach if he would be interested in you coming to the team once a week for ten minutes to give a series of talks on athletic motivation and challenges. You can mention some of the topics here or create your own. (For more on this see Appendix Seven.)

Using Team Huddles As An Outreach Tool

Somewhere during the season, and at the end if you are doing these talks weekly, have a special meeting with the athletes in one of their homes. Have a time of fun games and food. Then use Team Huddle Twelve (or another one if only talking to the team once) as your final talk to the students. Have a student share how God changed his life. Then end the meeting with an opportunity for students to choose the path to victory by beginning an eternal relationship with God.

You will either want to have students record what they thought of the meeting on comment cards or have flyers to invite them to a follow-up meeting on how to develop their relationship with God. Whatever you do, plan for it ahead of time and be ready at the outreach meeting to let students know how they can find out more about what you have presented to them.

Note To The Reader

There are a few more ideas in Appendix Seven that you will want to read about before you begin.

4

Writing and Giving Your Own Team Huddle

While you may want to simply use the Team Huddles presented in this book you can develop your own talks for your team. It is simple to do. Simply follow the outline below and you will have your talk!

Writing A Talk That Is Alive

Students need to re-live the experiences that you talk about. To do this you need to develop a talk that is Alive. The acrostic below describes the elements of a talk that is Alive.

Anecdote—I begin with a little known athletic story to focus the team on the topic.

Lesson—I simply state the single point that I want to make.

Illustrate—Give them an example of the point or principle in action.

Vision—Here is the fork in the road where you salt their spiritual interest and relate the point to their need for developing the spiritual dimension of their life. Remember: Make it short and clear.

Exercise—Give them something to do with what you told them.

Your talk will be five to seven minutes long if you have one point and one illustration as your opening story, one illustration after you bring out your point, and perhaps one illustration at the vision step. You can make the talk longer by repeating the A., L., and I steps (Anecdote, Lesson, and Illustration Steps). You can repeat these as many times as you need to for as many points as you want to make. But I would limit the total talk to ten to fifteen minutes at the most.

Since you are most likely focusing on only one key point, you may want to repeat steps A., L., and I for one or more of these four reasons: 1) You want to **emphasize** the point by repeating it using different stories and illustrations and then saying the key lesson in different terms. 2) You want to **prove** your point with another illustration and story. 3) You want to **explain** your point with another story and illustration. 4) You want to **apply** your point by telling another story and illustrating it. I have done some of each of these in the Team Huddles in this book.

If you play sports you should have some of your own illustrations for a talk. You may want to use illustrations from this book or you can find your own in other books, magazines, and even on the sports segments of the news on radio or TV. Keep your ears open for interesting and humorous stories. When you hear one write it down. You may decide to develop a talk around some of the stories you collect.

As an athlete you have learned several lessons that all of your teammates need to hear, too. Think about what lessons you believe are important and keep a journal of them. If you decide to develop one as a talk you will need that illustration file I just talked about.

Giving A Talk That Is Alive

Your own personal stories are very good to use. But when you tell any story always give enough detail so those who are listening can re-live the experience with you. Paint a picture for them as you speak. Don't give away a surprise ending until the ending. If you can find a humorous story to tell use it. Then state the reason you used that story and the point it makes. The point it makes should be the point you wanted to make at the beginning.

Know your talk well enough to do it from memory. If your talk is based upon stories—and it is—then know each of the stories. They should not be hard to recall. The hard part will be remembering the order and the key point(s). After learning the stories know where you want to make your point(s) and think through how you want to say them. You can use a memory tool like an acrostic to recall the order of things in your talk. I have already given you the acrostic A.L.I.V.E. If you just follow this each time you will know what to say and when. As your talk gets more complicated you may need to memorize the points and place the stories and illustrations around them. You could also develop another acrostic to help you through the talk.

If you need to use note cards just place on one 3x5 card a brief outline of the talk. Note on it the key points and the name of the illustration at each point. This can also help you get through it or it will come in handy if you get stuck during the talk.

Pray through the preparation of the talk. Trust God with your delivery of it. Remember, He is the one in the audience. Give it for Him and let your teammates enjoy listening to your conversation with Him.

5

Using Team Huddles as a Discipleship Tool

Throughout these Huddles the basics of the faith are covered in the Time Out sections. It begins with a look at the importance of the spiritual area of our lives as compared to the physical, mental, and social areas. Then it moves into dealing with sin in our lives as believers. In Huddle Three we cover how to have the power to live the Christian life on a daily basis. The fourth Huddle deals with what we think and how that affects us. The fifth Huddle looks at who we do things for and directs us to do all things for God. The sixth Huddle deals with peer pressure and living with a clear conscience as we make good decisions. Huddle seven covers Knowing God, spending daily time with Him and what believers can do when they know Him. Huddle eight deals with Lordship and living sacrificially. Huddle nine looks at our identity in Christ. The tenth Huddle covers assurance of salvation. Huddle eleven focuses upon being open and honest in our times with God. And the last Huddle covers the area of living by faith and being a witness to others.

All of these topics are covered in the Time Out sections. Simply by taking a student through these Time Out sections can help him grow as a believer and become Christ-like in thought and action. You could offer this study as a follow-up to your talks to the team. You may want to offer them at the end of the season for only 4-6 weeks. If you do this you will have to pick which Huddles you will cover and which ones you will not cover at this time. I would suggest that you do Huddles 1-3 and 10 for a four week series. If you want to make the initial study six weeks then include Team Huddle seven and eleven. After that time you can offer another study for those who would like to continue with you and finish the Team Huddles. Make sure each student has a copy of the book. Ask them to read the Huddle and do the Time Out before coming to your meeting. Or, read the Huddle before coming and do the Time Out together. You will also find that the students can do the Time Outs on their own and then you simply need to develop a guided discussion that covers the same subject but in a more in-depth manner.

6

Sharing Your Faith

Sharing your faith is a step of faith that every believer needs to take. It is the opportunity to help another student or adult choose the path to victory. It is the most joyful experience that a believer can ever have when they see a person step out of darkness and into light and begin an eternal relationship with the living God.

Sharing Your Faith Using A Tool

You can share your faith simply by reading a tool like the booklet called, "Would you like to know God personally?" to a person. You can also simply turn to Appendix One and ask a person if they have an eternal relationship with God. Then ask if you can get their opinion of the two pages in your Team Huddle book. Simply read the material and pause when it asks a question. Give them time to respond then continue. Ask them if they would like to pray the prayer at the end of the material. Remind them that the written prayer is only there to help direct their thoughts and it is the attitude of their heart that is important. The prayer is simply worded to help them express to God their desire to know Him.

If they don't respond do not be discouraged. Let them know that they will probably want to do it someday in the future. Make a copy of Appendix One to give them. Or, if you used a booklet then give that to them. (To order the suggested booklet contact Integrated Resources at 1-800-729-4351.)

Using Your Testimony To Share Your Faith

You will want to develop and use your personal experience of coming to faith in God at some time. Here is how to develop your personal testimony.

First, write down what your life was like before you came to Christ or before you made Him Lord of your life if you came to Christ at a young age.

Second, write down how you came to Christ. Make it clear enough that another person listening to you could also make the decision you made to receive Christ. (If you came to Christ early, share how and when you made Christ Lord of your life.)

Finally, write down what God has done in your life since you have come to Christ or made Him Lord of your life. Close with a verse from the Bible that relates to the theme of your testimony or simply share your favorite verse.

Your entire testimony should last about three minutes and should be memorized. You may have more to say and there are times when an expanded testimony is fine to give however, for an outreach situation where you are not the main speaker at an event or in the midst of a presentation of the gospel, you will want to keep it short and to the point.

Trust God to give you opportunities to share your testimony with others as a way of life. After you share it don't forget to ask the other person if they would like to begin an eternal relationship with God. If they would like to, simply lead them in prayer and ask them to make what you pray their own. Make sure that what you say indicates that they are asking for Christ to come into their lives, forgive their sin, and make them the person God created them to be.

Remember, talk to God about men before you talk to men about God. In other words, pray at all times.

7

A Challenge to Youth Workers

"Let's bring it in," calls the coach. He says a few words to the team and then turns to you. "Men, I want you to give your attention to our speaker today."

Another high school football season has begun. But this season will be different for you and for the team. You now have ten to twelve minutes each week to challenge and motivate them.

SOWING TO REAP

Speaking to student athletes is not new to me. I often give one of two or three talks to each of the athletic teams at a school during a year. Then I meet with the students who indicate that they have an interest in the spiritual area of their life.

Conducting Team Huddles is different. I was committing myself to give or "have brought in" ten or more different talks for the same group of students!

My goal was not to just find those students who were interested in spiritual things, but to actually increase interest that had not yet developed. This required much more prayer. I not only was bringing students a key athletic principle but also a spiritual lesson that could only be successfully applied under God's power. As I prayed for the students and the talks I asked God to use them to bring the students into a personal relationship with Him.

INCREASING AWARENESS

One student had been to 46 Huddles during his high school football career but had not come to Christ. I asked him later at the end of his senior year what the Huddles had done for him. He said, "Before you came I never thought about God, but now I'm open to Him."

Each Huddle is designed to take biblical principles, present them as they relate to athletics, and end with a challenge. I then mention at the end that these principles can only be consistently applied once the spiritual area of their life is given proper attention.

In the book, *What's Gone Wrong With The Harvest?*, the writers note how a person moves from an awareness of a Supreme Being to the gospel and then to a decision for Christ.[1] I discovered that God was using these weekly ten minute Huddles to move students from a lack of awareness of God all the way to a decision for Christ.

CHANGED LIVES

I was meeting with over 100 students and coaches each week at a school in Pennsylvania. At the end of the first season I gave the students an opportunity to hear more about the spiritual area of their lives. About 15 students indicated they would like to talk with me.

Eleven of these students indicated they wanted to develop a

relationship with God. When I called Kraig to ask him why he had indicated a desire to know God on his comment card he said, "My parents don't go to church, so I thought you could help me with it."

Kraig was a starting fullback. For the next five years every fullback on the team came to Christ. There was Stu, then Tim. Tim even made eleven touchdowns during his senior year, was elected King of his senior prom, and went to state in three track events. When writing his paragraph for the year book he didn't mention any of these things, instead he wrote:

> Thanks Mom and Mike. Even youths grow tired and weary, and young men stumble and fall; But those who hope in the Lord will renew their strength. They will soar on wings like eagles. Isa. 40:30-31

During Tim's senior year, he was able to speak to the winter track team (about 55 students), share his faith in Christ and challenge them to consider our Lord. Also that year we saw the entire starting line-up for the football team come to Christ. At the beginning of the season we knew of twelve who were believers, but 21 others came to Christ as a result of the Huddle series.

LARGEST TARGET GROUP

Every school has two different kinds of campus groups. There are activity groups where students come together because they like the same sport or club. There is also the social network of friends. This last group may cross many activity groups.

When football season begins, there can be more than 100 players involved in the sport. Some schools may even have more if they field a freshman, sophomore, junior varsity or reserve, and a varsity team. This makes this activity group one of the largest groupings of guys at one time anywhere on the campus. As a result, there are also many social networks of friends within it.

SET-UP

I was once told, "You will never accomplish anything unless you place yourself in a situation where you have to act." I do work best when I've scheduled an activity that I have to do. So I began with prayer and then took action. Prayer always results in action.

Before I had everything "just right" and with only three athletic talks prepared, I went into the coach's office. I asked him if he would be interested in having a series of ten to twelve minute motivational talks given to his team before each game. Each talk would focus on the physical, social, mental and spiritual areas of an athlete's development. Later I asked if I could give them a few moments at the end of each talk to apply what I had told them.

My first contact with the coach indicated that he was doing some of these things with the team already. So I also offered to bring in former football players and some professionals to speak to the team. By the following season we began weekly chapels or team huddles before each game.

RESOURCES

For the first couple of years I made use of many other college, former high school, and former professional football players as speakers at the chapels or huddles. Later, I used these contacts only once or twice during a season and did most of the talks myself.

If you have the resources to bring in other athletes that is a great way to run the Huddles as long as you are the one who introduces each speaker. If you have a sensitive situation then make sure your speakers will not "blow you out of the water" with what they say.

TIMING

Every coach has a different style of leading his team. For some they will want the talk just before the game on the day of the game. Others will want it the day before the game on the short day of practice.

Also, you will need to find out if he wants it before practice or at the end. Be ready to flex because practices do not end on time, and if they get out early you may miss your chance to speak.

TRAINING OTHERS

When I moved to a new city I decided to introduce the Huddle strategy to our staff. They began trying it. We did not have many resources to draw upon. So, most of the talks needed to be done by the staff. That was when I began getting visits from staff to go through my Huddle illustration file. Some used these illustrations to put together their own talks while some of my talks were borrowed and used.

As you prepare your talks, make sure you keep a file of all your athletic illustrations. If you played football or another sport you may already have some good illustrations. But if not, read sports stories and illustrations of the lives of other athletes and you will soon have plenty of illustrations as well as ideas for talks.

TALK PREPARATION

I use a simple formula for preparing talks for the Huddles. It follows the acrostic ALIVE.

Students learn best when they can live out the lesson. So, this method is illustration heavy.

<u>A</u>necdote—I begin with a little known athletic story to focus the team on the topic.

<u>L</u>esson—I simply state the single point that I want to make.

<u>I</u>llustrate—Give them an example of the point or principle in action.

<u>V</u>ision—Here is the fork in the road where you salt their spiritual interest and relate the point to their need for developing the spiritual dimension of their life. Remember: Make it short and clear.

<u>E</u>xercise—Give them something to do with what you told them.

You may have more than one point in the Lesson stage. (Remember to illustrate each one.) But with only ten or twelve minutes it is best to limit your challenge to one point, and work on giving the athletic stories in a way that they can experience them as you tell each one.

CONDUCTING A TEAM HUDDLE

I have not been consistent in how I begin a Team Huddle.

Sometimes I have a few short comments before I start my talk. Once I gave them the top five questions asked by those on the bench. One question was, "Does Pizza Hut deliver to the bench?"

Almost always I begin with a story and this is where the talk starts. I often use stories about football even back into the late 1800s. That started some students guessing about the year of my illustrations before each Team Huddle.

At the end I give the students one minute to quietly think about the talk. Then I close in prayer—I usually do this part even if the team heard someone else speak.

CLOSING THE SEASON

Towards the last Team Huddle I make use of comment cards. First I ask the coach if I can get the students' reaction to the Huddle series, then I give the students an opportunity to tell me what they thought. I always appreciate a student who will stand behind his comments by putting his name on the card— not his friend who is not there.

Make sure you ask specifically for their names and phone numbers, if you use this method. However, you can invite them to an all team meeting instead of using comment cards.

Set a time the next day (or within that week) for every one on the team to come for pizza and soda. At the group meeting you can give the gospel, have an athlete's testimony, and then make use of comment cards. This meeting can easily take place in one of the students' homes. Whatever you do make sure you meet with them off campus and give the students an opportunity to receive Christ.

Once at the last Huddle of the season I discovered that the

coach had a tradition with the seniors that kept me from doing a Huddle that day. I was glad I had done the cards the week before. So, don't wait until the end and be surprised that your key talk was not able to be given to the team.

You may find that the coach will want the Huddle series to be optional. This may cut those attending from 100 to twenty or less. But, the year we saw 21 of the starters come to Christ was the year we had to move our Huddles off campus and into a student's home. One student even said, "I always play better when I come to the chapels." He was not kidding!

Remember, you are just offering what most pro teams are already doing!.

For more help on working with students visit the Coaching Center at www.gocampus.org or call 1-877-GOCAMPUS.

---

[1] James F. Engel and H. Wilbert Norton, <u>What's Gone Wrong With The Harvest?</u> (Zondervan Publishing House: Grand Rapids, 1975) p. 45.